Francisque Sarcey

Recollections of middle life

Translated by Elisabeth Luther Cary

Francisque Sarcey

Recollections of middle life
Translated by Elisabeth Luther Cary

ISBN/EAN: 9783337127060

Printed in Europe, USA, Canada, Australia, Japan

Cover: Foto ©ninafisch / pixelio.de

More available books at **www.hansebooks.com**

RECOLLECTIONS OF MIDDLE LIFE

RECOLLECTIONS OF MIDDLE LIFE

BY

FRANCISQUE SARCEY

TRANSLATED FROM THE FRENCH BY

ELISABETH LUTHER CARY

LONDON
WILLIAM HEINEMANN
1893
[*All rights reserved*]

Introduction

THE reader of this volume will be likely to get a definite impression of its author, for M. Francisque Sarcey has a very distinct personality, a very lively consciousness of it, and remarkable candor in referring to it. It is an interesting personality in many ways, and to a reader with the good sense to enjoy the unusual frankness of its manifestations, and the good-humor to overlook some of the more extreme, the book will bring new light on some phases of French life not often easily studied. M. Sarcey has been teacher, journalist, dramatic critic, novelist, lecturer, and for more than thirty years an eager and fortunate member of that society in Paris which embraces men of letters, artists, and the extremely varied class for whom *esprit* opens most, if not all, doors. In these pages will be found much, sometimes important and significant, and always interesting, as to this curious and engaging world, *le monde où l'on s'amuse*, but in which there is far more hard work, vigorous purpose, and sober thought than the English-speaking reader commonly suspects. It may be that my own occupation has led me to value more highly at once the instruction and the charm of M. Sarcey's book than would the general reader, but it at least gives me a modest claim to attention for the statement, that a young man wishing to make journalism his calling can find in this volume some rules that he would do well to study, many suggestions that ought to be useful to him, and a lesson of patient industry, of constant conscientiousness, of sturdy independence and self-respect, and of invincible good-will, that can hardly fail to stimulate and strengthen whatever there is of good in him. With this hint as to what it seems to me that the little work may offer to its readers, it remains only to give an outline of the principal facts in M. Sarcey's career.

He was born in 1828, at Dourdan, in the Department of Seine-et-Oise, and had his schooling at the Lycée Charlemagne, winning honors in common with Edmond About, who was to be his life-long friend, and to exert a decisive influence over his course in later years. He entered the École Normale in 1848, still with About, and with H. Taine, and H. d'Audegier. At this time he had a notion that he was born to be a musician and composer, and made efforts of heroic obstinacy to fulfil his fancied mission. He came reluctantly to the conclusion that he was mistaken, and obtained an appointment in the Department of Public Instruction as professor of the third class, his first assignment being to Chaumont. But at the outset of his career he gave serious offence to the authorities by an extravagant remonstrance against the order requiring professors to cut off their mustaches, and he never overcame the effect of this youthful "manifestation." He was banished to remote and unimportant stations — Lesneven (Finisterre), Rodez, Grenoble — and passed, with difficulty and slowly, through the grades to that of Professor of Philosophy. Of philosophy M. Sarcey has, as the reader will see, a varied and useful store, but it hardly seems of the pedagogic sort.

In 1859, when the Empire was at the height of its glory abroad, and had reached the lowest depth of its meddlesome despotism at home, M. Sarcey got a year's leave of absence from duty and went to Paris, as nearly every young man of ambition was sure to do, and, as all such young men were apt to do, tried his hand at journalism. By About's friendly offices he found work on *Le Figaro*, and during the next year continued his labors there and on numerous other journals. In 1860, About called him to take the work of dramatic criticism on *L'Opinion nationale*, in which, as he modestly says, "the most of my little fame has come to me." He resigned his professorship, not without acute regret, for it had given him "some of the sweetest pleasures of life," and he is able to say that he believes he was "a good, and even a rare, professor." Dramatic criticism was, however, to become his profession, and he followed it with rigid method, with great industry, and with deserved success. No drudgery was too tedious for him. He saw every play he wrote of, not only once, but many times, and faithfully and minutely studied every player. "I love the theatre," he wrote, "with so absolute a love, that I sacrifice everything, even my personal friendships, and, what is still more difficult, my repugnances, to the pleasure of urging the crowd to a play that seems to me good, or away from one that seems to me bad."

He did not confine himself, however, to this work, but contributed various articles besides to his own and to other journals. In 1867 he joined the staff of *Le Temps*, and afterward that of *Le Gaulois*, and when this journal, after the war, became Imperialist, he went with About to the newly established *Dix-neuvième Siècle*. He had the usual varied experience of the French journalist, fought the regulation duel, was sued and fined, and passed his fifteen days in prison, *à propos* of an imprudent discussion of *Les Bouchons de l'eau de Lourdes*. But his career was, on the whole, as successful and happy as it was busy and laborious. He found time to write several ro-

Introduction

mances, "Le Nouveau Seigneur de Village," a satire on the Imperial mayors; "Étienne Monet, Roman psychologique;" "Le Piano de Jeanne;" "Qui Perd Gagne;" "Il ne faut jamais dire, Fontaine." He wrote an amusing and very ingenious little volume "Le Mot et la Chose," tracing the different meanings of familiar words at successive periods and among different classes; a story of the Siege of Paris; an essay critical and biographic on "Paul-Louis Courier, Écrivain;" a collection of sketches "Comédiens et Comédiennes;" and in 1885, the autobiographic volume, "Souvenirs de Jeunesse," of which the present is a sequel.

It will be seen that his "literary baggage" is not inconsiderable, while the volume of his work in the journals is, of course, enormous.

In 1889 he seriously considered whether he should present his claims, which were by no means weak, to a seat in the Academy; but, with rare discernment, resolved not to do so. In explaining his course, he said: "I have but one ambition; it is that on my tomb-stone may be placed the inscription, summing up my life: Sarcey, Professor and Journalist." In another place, he wrote: "I have no pretention to style, or better, I have but one. Boileau, in speaking of himself, has said,

Et mon vers, bien ou mal, dit toujours quelque chose.

As for me, my phrase, well or ill, always says something." The reader of these "Souvenirs" will readily verify this judgment. I find it as correct as it is sincere, and, because it is so, this curious and minute and ample account of the author's experiences, methods, failures, and achievements appears to me to justify itself. To paraphrase his remark *à propos* of his first lecture at the Athénée: "The reader who seeks a writer will find a man."

EDWARD CARY.

Contents

	PAGE
Introduction, ...	*v*
I.	*1*
II. *My Début as a Lecturer,* . .	*3*
III. *At the Athénée-Comique,* . . .	25
IV. *The Lectures at the Athénée,* . .	44
V. *The First Ballande Matinée,* .	61
VI. *The Ballande Matinées Before 1870,*	78
VII. *The Ballande Matinées After 1870,*	93
VIII. *How to Lecture,* . . .	*136*
IX. *How a Lecture is Prepared,* . .	*156*
X. *In the Provinces,*	*173*
XI. *In Foreign Lands,*	*193*

Contents

	PAGE
XII. In Holland,	210
XIII. At the Salle des Capucines,	228
XIV. Difficulties of the Enterprise,	247
XV. On the Manner of Giving Lectures upon Books,	268
XVI. Decadence of the Lectures of the Boulevard des Capucines,	291
Notes,	303

RECOLLECTIONS OF MIDDLE LIFE

I.

There are those who have appeared to desire that I should add a volume to that in which I told the story of my childhood and my youth, and my amiable publisher, by whom the first part of my memoirs had been issued, urged me, in the most friendly manner, to commence a new series of them. I hesitated a long time; memories which date from that delightful springtime of life have, naturally, a grace and freshness most often wanting to those of maturity. The too favorable reception that the public had been good enough to give to my first volume, far from encouraging me, filled me with distrust. Some years have passed over my head since it was written. Could I recall, at will, that fine temper of the mind and that gayety of language that made the success of the earlier narrative? I do not feel, thank

Heaven! any bitterness toward life, which has always been kindly to me. But the time is past of that happy, causeless laughter that jets spontaneously from a well balanced soul in a robust body. What matter! I will try once more.

I shall open to you a little corner of my life in Paris; I am going to show you how I became a lecturer, and what, to my mind, a lecture is. If you take pleasure in this study—which will be short—I shall continue; I shall tell you of my years of journalism. If not, we will stop there.

II.

MY DÉBUT AS A LECTURER

I had already made something of a name for myself in the press as theatrical critic, *chroniqueur*, reviewer, what-not? for I am used to working with equal ardor at all things that concern my trade; it had not yet entered my mind that I could join to the profession of journalist that of lecturer. For this there was an excellent reason: the lecture did not exist in Paris, and the word "lecturer" was as unknown there as was, three or four years ago, that of "interviewer."

We knew, by hearsay, that in England some celebrated writers did not disdain to seat themselves before a glass of sweetened water, manuscript in hand, and to read therefrom a certain number of pages to an audience gathered expressly to listen to them. But that, properly speaking, was not a lecture. Dickens had come to Paris to give some of these readings, which were attended by hardly anyone save the English colony. We were too ill-acquainted with Shakespeare's tongue to pay twenty-five francs for the very problematical pleasure of staring at a great writer.

We had been told that in Belgium some of our political refugees, and first among them M. Deschanel, driven to the sad necessity of gaining their living, no matter how, had introduced there the entirely novel art of lecturing.

They bore from town to town their lessons, or rather their talks, which the population, and especially the feminine part of the population, flocked eagerly to hear. But we had few details as to this innovation, and we said to ourselves that though it had succeeded in Belgium, where the people have more time for reflection and for tedium, it had few chances of becoming acclimated in Paris where only amusing distractions are liked. Between the Sorbonne lesson, or that of the College of France, and evening conversation in *salon* or *atelier*, we did not suspect that there could be a place for an exercise of speech having a relation to each, not too serious nor too frivolous, and which might become for good society a recreation of high order.

The first essays in lecturing took place at Paris in the month of May, 1860, in a great hall which the organizers had rented in the Rue de la Paix. The purpose of these gentlemen was, I believe, somewhat political.

My Début as a Lecturer

In the vast silence of the Empire their idea was to found a tribune where one could, insinuatingly, quietly, under cover of history or literature, launch epigrams against the government. As I had always professed a complete scepticism regarding politics, caring neither to ally myself to the imperial régime, nor to combat it, I had never been thought of, and had received no proposition to fill that improvised chair, nor should I have consented to do so.

The sessions at which I had been present by chance were not attractive. I had there seen my poor school-mate, Alfred Assolant, now dead, make his *début* in lecturing. Assolant had always thrown himself passionately into politics; on December 2d, he, professor in a city of the provinces, had gone down into the public square and called the citizens to arms.

How came it that after this generous outburst he was neither shot nor sent into exile? As to that I know less than nothing! He had refused the oath, given in his resignation, and had come to live by his pen in Paris. His first book, "Scenes of Life in the United States," which is a masterpiece of French "go" and British humor, had obtained an enormous success, and had brought him at once to the fore.

He was a singular fellow, who joined to a rare

boldness of soul an incredible timidity of manner. These two qualities would seem to exclude one another—in him they were found together. He was endowed with a strong and tenacious will; when once he had reached a resolution, and his resolutions were always excessive, he pushed on to the end with an invincible obstinacy. Once we saw him stand for a seat in the *Corps législatif*, in his native department where he was no longer known to any one. All his friends dissuaded him from this sword-thrust in water, which would make him ridiculous. Nothing stopped him; he wrote article upon article, sent circulars, begged us all to patronize his candidacy, and harvested twelve votes. Astonished at the result, but undismayed, he talked of starting in again at the following elections.

He took himself off, his eye lost in space, his hat far back on a brow already very bald, his long legs divided like compasses, in pursuit of his dream, disdainful of obstacles, energetic and headstrong. Withal timid — timid to a degree you cannot imagine. He never could find the word he wanted to use; without a shadow of repartee, he had not even staircase wit. About amused himself with disconcerting him, and nothing was easier, alas! for at the slightest attack he stammered or grew angry. But for the most part he shut himself up against pleasantry—he who, pen in hand, could counter so readily—in a bristling silence. I do not believe that he ever in his life finished a phrase in conversation.

It was precisely this war against the impossible that tempted him. Nature had refused him the speaker's gift, and he determined to be an orator. When he was applied to for a lecture in the Rue de la Paix, he did not weigh the matter for an instant, and what was more amusing, having consented to run this risk, he did not even think of putting all possible chances in his favor. He seated himself for the first time in the lecturer's chair with an ingenuousness of confidence that is intelligible only to those who knew this inconsequent and contradictory being. He had taken for his theme the title of his book: "La Vie aux États-Unis."

"Gentlemen," he said, with an assured air, "when one desires to set out for America—for America—when one desires to go there—one takes the boat—it is necessary to take the boat." His audience listened to him somewhat nonplussed. Suddenly we saw him gather up his papers, his book, rise to his feet, descend from the chair. "And I—I take the door!" he cried. A wild laugh ran along the tiers, no, not tiers, there was but one, which by good fortune was filled with friends.

That lecture became legendary, like the one given

one evening by the celebrated Bohemian, Pelloquet, who arrived more than half drunk with one of his friends, who had drunk as much as he, and as the words fell slowly from his thick tongue:

"Go in, ol' fellow," said his comrade to him in an encouraging voice, "give it to 'em straight."

The second lecture at which I was present in the hall of the Rue de la Paix was that of Gaston de Saint-Valry. I take pleasure in recalling this name, now nearly forgotten by the public. He is one of the men in our profession for whom I have had the liveliest esteem, and I believed him called to a great future. He possessed very varied and very profound learning, which he preferred to let glimmer through his articles, rather than to unfold it, having about him not a shade of pedantry. He had a horror of "snobs," and met them with a haughty disdain. He was a philosopher, and carried into his literary criticism, or into current politics, rare gifts as a moralist; he wrote in a sober and firm style, and his prose was always full of sense.

Unfortunately he only worked on journals without circulation. It did not displease him to be read but by a small number of good minds. There was at that time a newspaper, founded by M. Poggenpol, called *Le Nord*, that aspired to competition with *l'Indépendance Belge*, which, if you remember, all

My Début as a Lecturer

Europe read under the Empire. As I contributed to it, I received it and read it assiduously. I had remarked some articles, which appeared three times a week, signed with a simple omega; I had been greatly struck with the variety and delicacy of the observations in which the pen of the anonymous writer abounded, his vigor of thought and his precision of language had charmed me. One day I met Gaston de Saint-Valry, with whom I was on good terms of literary comradeship, for he loved the theatre and liked to talk of it.

"You know all Paris secrets," I said to him, "tell me who signs himself in *Le Nord* with an omega. He is a moralist of originality and a masterly writer."

Not a muscle of his face stirred.

"I will ask Poggenpol about it," he answered me.

I learned afterward from M. Poggenpol himself that it was Gaston de Saint-Valry who, through hatred of stupid publicity, and in order also to be freer in his criticisms, screened his personality with that initial.

Quite the opposite of Assolant, Gaston de Saint-Valry talked with fluency and force, he spoke with decision in an imperious and cutting voice, the right word left his lips like an arrow. Thus it did not astonish me when he informed me that he was going to give a lecture.

He was an imperialist, or rather, in politics, a convinced and determined believer in authority. It was not unpleasing to him to carry to that tribune, where the opposition amused itself with the pin pricks of a teasing liberalism, ideas flowing from another doctrine. He begged me to attend, and I did not fail to do so, for I liked and admired him with all my heart. I believed he would sweep his public off their feet. What a disappointment awaited me! This robust talker, who in conversation knew so well what he wanted to say, and who said it so directly and so clearly, could no longer find his words; he hemmed and hawed, he lost the thread of his argument, and in order to regain it he was obliged to recur to his notes, and in these he lost his way.

It was a painful hour both for him and for us. As he had no foolish vanity, and was unassuming, we discussed this gloomy failure freely. He told me of the singular impression the audience had made on him; he was unprepared; he had been frightened, and had lost his head. It was not such a very terrible audience either. There were not more than sixty persons in that vast hall, and all these persons knew him; he could count on their sympathy. It was of no use! He could not control his emotion;

My Début as a Lecturer

the lecture, all prepared, had fled in confusion from his memory.

"It is," I told him, "what the comedians call in their *argot* the '*trac*.'"

"It is one of the most disagreeable sensations in the world, and I shall not expose myself to it a second time."

"Nevertheless, your ambition is to reach the Chamber."

"Oh! the Chamber, that's another matter. One is there face to face with political adversaries who interrupt—who talk back. It seems to me that there I should be at ease."

But Gaston de Saint-Valry was to speak no more, either in the Chamber or in the Rue de la Paix, for he was mown down in the full force of years and talent, and his loss is one of the most poignant that have fallen to contemporary journalism.

These examples would have sufficed to repress in me all desire to attempt lecturing if at heart the desire had really tormented me. The truth is that I did not think for a moment of it.

The lectures of the Rue de la Paix had never made much noise in the Parisian world. They changed their place without the public being warned of it by the ghost of a *lettre de faire part*. There had been speaking in the Rue de la Paix before a small audience of friends. Then the speaking was resumed in the Rue Scribe, before the same audience. The great public took no notice.

And nevertheless, the idea of establishing lectures had, in an obscure fashion, made its way. It was in the air, as we say nowadays. Lectures with the ulterior idea of a political propaganda had failed, as was nearly inevitable under the régime by which we were stifled. Those who dreamed vaguely of reviving the institution took it up on another side. There was quite a notion at that period (for the Emperor affected to be the first socialist of his time) of enlightening the people, spreading instruction, all kinds of instruction, through the masses.

The neutrality, and perhaps even the good will, of the powers that were, apt though they were to take umbrage, was secure, if the lecture were merely confined to an intellectual recreation for the middle class, with the reputed purpose of familiarizing them with the progress of the sciences, with new ideas in literature or in art.

One fine morning Felix Hément appeared at my house.

Felix Hément, who has since occupied in the University the high post of General Inspector of Primary Instruction, and who, after having lived withdrawn from all honors, but always enamoured of teaching,

My Début as a Lecturer

has just died at Nanterre, was at the time I knew him half-professor, half-journalist.

He was a man who was very correct in manner and dress, with a clear and amiable voice, endowed with a marvellous facility in elocution, and whose hobby (and a noble one withal) it had always been to render science accessible to all, lending to it all the graces of his language, touching, as our fathers used to say, the edge of the vase with honey.

He became, later on, one of the happiest and most ardent promoters of those pedagogic lectures which have, in the provinces, rendered such great service to free thought and to primary teaching. But he was young at that time, unknown and without authority; this project for reviving a taste for the things of the mind by the free lecture boiled in his brain, and escaped at hazard in diffused and vague vapors. It was not yet clearly and precisely formulated.

I had formed a friendship with him through Millaud, the manager of the *Petit Journal*, and of twenty other papers born of that one. I worked in that mill under the orders of the chief, whose nephew or cousin he was, I no longer remember exactly which. I had appreciated the extent of his information, his rectitude of judgment, and, above all, the taste for pedagogy common to us both. I felt in him a devotee who performed his devotions in the chapel whither my thoughts ceaselessly led me.

He had explained to me that he had rented on the Quai Malaquais a large hall, where he planned to give three or four lectures a week—one on science, another on literature, another on history. It was a kind of free philosophical institute, for there was to be no sustained course, but each lecturer would try to awaken in his hearers new ideas on the subject chosen. He hoped that the women of the *bourgeoisie* would come to these sessions, and that they would bring their daughters.

He proposed to me to open the literary series with a lecture on Corneille. I saw in it only a class to take and I accepted without resistance, sure of myself, since I was taking up again for a day the calling of professor, which I had exercised for ten years.

The recollection of that first lecture will remain eternally graven on my memory. It was a Monday in December. Toward three o'clock in the afternoon the clouds, which since morning had dragged, dingy and gray, over Paris, burst, and the snow commenced to fall with silent regularity in great flakes, thick and close. Toward six o'clock traffic ceased, the streets were impassable and all the coachmen took their carriages to the stables.

"I shall never get there," I said to myself, look-

My Début as a Lecturer

ing through the window-panes at the veil of flat whiteness which united earth and sky. And I was not sorry either.

I began to find that I had given my word to Félix Hément very lightly. It was not so easy as I had believed to talk of Corneille an hour running to a strange audience. Chance came of itself to my succor by keeping the audience away.

I set out on foot. On the quays the snow was knee-deep, and at most one could perceive at wide distances against that vast white shroud a black form detach itself, a witness in the wide silence of the deserted street that the city was not dead.

I arrived exhausted and soaked. There were five persons altogether in the hall, among them Félix Hément and his secretary; two friends of mine who had braved that Siberian temperature to listen to me. I never knew the name of the fifth, of that heroic fifth whom I cannot compare to the fifth wheel of a coach, since he was alone my entire audience, the others not counting.

Was he pleased? Wert thou pleased, brave and consoling Fifth, who, like Joab's wise woman, hast never told thy name, and hast never been seen again? I have carried thee long in my heart, and keep a grateful corner in my memory for thee. I no longer recall whether I spoke well or ill that evening, but it was for thee I spoke, and when "Gentlemen" escaped me, it was to thee that I in my gratitude addressed that polite plural.

Félix Hément paid me, as he was obliged in courtesy to do, many compliments, but we did not renew the experiment. The snow lasted long enough that year of ill luck. The hearers we had counted on preferred to remain in the corner by the fire.

"*Et le combat finit faute de combatants.*"

I had forgotten this incident, and thought no more of lectures, when, one evening at the theatre, I was approached by a young man whose long hair fell over his shoulders, whose large, fine eyes, wide open and full of fire, his amiable smile and melodious voice, won me from the first. He abounded in gestures, and the words flowed from his mouth as water from a fountain, without pause or interruption, in harmonious sound.

He told me that he was a lawyer, that he was commencing to try his hand at journalism, but that his ambition, his real and ardent ambition, was to restore, or rather to establish, the lecture in our country. I regarded him with curiosity; he appeared to me very young to have conceived such a project and to carry it to completion.

My Début as a Lecturer

It was M. de Lapommeraye. In the course of this recital I shall very often have to talk with you of Lapommeraye, for during long years we lectured together in brotherly fashion at Paris in the same halls; together we traversed the provinces and foreign parts, where our two names are still associated in the same memories. But he had this advantage over me —he entered lecturing, by definite choice, at an age when one can still serve apprenticeship at a trade. Scarcely out of college, at twenty years of age, he had said to himself, " I will be a lay preacher for ladies." It is an art for which he had an instinct. He had only to concern himself with the handling and the practice. He had from the very first—what is so rare in life—put his finger on his vocation.

Was I born to lecture? It must indeed be believed that I had some aptitude for it, since, after all, I have had much success and have made myself a name in it. But I never prepared myself by any study. People in general believe readily that one learns to speak by practice at the teacher's desk. Nothing of the kind; one has no need of eloquence in a class, and I would almost venture to say that eloquence there is mischievous. A professor who likes to talk, and who talks too much, is nearly always a pretty bad professor.

One obtains command over one's pupils less by

alluring them with grace or charm of discourse—for discourse is only used very intermittently in classes—than by having the air of believing profoundly what one teaches them, and interesting one's self ardently in what they do. To believe and to love, you see, that's all there is of a professor.

When I go over in my mind my college years, I see that the masters who had the most influence over me were precisely those who were not *beaux esprits*, who did not know how to string elegant phrases. It was Caboche who first opened to me the secret of the language of the seventeenth century. This worthy man had a very narrow mind, and he had never in his life been able to complete a sentence; but when in his nasal voice he read us two lines of Pascal or of Bossuet, his two favorite writers, and when stopping at each member of the period, he said, with a way of turning his right hand admiringly, "That is beautiful, my friends, that is beautiful!" there flashed in his gesture and in his voice a conviction so strong that we ourselves were seized with enthusiasm and we repeated, "Oh, yes, that is beautiful!" And we found out why it was beautiful, for one always finds good reasons to justify one's sentiment to one's self.

Sainte-Beuve somewhere ridicules an old-style professor of the old University, who, reading to his pupils the story of Laocoön in the second book of the

Æneid, adorned it with commentaries after the ancient fashion:

"*Ecce autem a Tenedo gemini tranquilla per alta.*"

"*Ecce*," said he, with admiration, "there they are—it is they—one sees them coming down there from the isle of Tenedos; *gemini*, coupled they swim. The poet did not use *ambo: ambo* would not be strong enough, they are not merely two, these two monsters, impelled by the same god; they direct themselves together toward one end, thirsting for the same murder, *tranquilla per alta*. Ah, gentlemen, nature knows nothing of the vengeance that they contemplate, the sea that they cleave is tranquil, and however high it is — *alta !* it cannot stop them!" And he continued in this tone verse upon verse.

Sainte-Beuve enjoys his laugh, and perhaps indeed there is a little simpleness and pedantry in these explanations. But they had one merit, the child who heard them, captivated by this air of conviction, kindled by this fire, left the class admiring with all his heart and with all his strength the verses of Virgil, fragments of which he carried in his memory

A philosophical dissertation on the Laocoön of sculpture, compared to that of poetry, would perchance have lent itself to the employment of brilliant eloquence, but nothing of it would have remained in the mind of the student. He would have gone out of the class full of admiration for the *bel esprit* of the professor, as a devout woman goes from the sermon of her *curé*, who prides himself on his eloquence. "He has spoken well to-day," says she, with a satisfied air. Do not ask her what he has said; she knows nothing of it. She has been moved by a vain sound of words.

I have exercised, I believe, and it is one of my sweetest recollections, a strong influence over some of the pupils whom chance has gathered year by year around my chair. I do not recall a single day when I have given a developed lesson when I have been eloquent, or, to put it plainly, a fine talker. I believed in the literature that I taught, I loved my pupils for the love of that; it seems to me that seriously I have been a very good professor, and even a rare professor. You will pardon me this little excess of retrospective vanity. But I never in my class trained myself to the art of speech, I knew nothing of this trade of lecturer for which Lapommeraye prepared himself in public disputes with future advocates.

He had managed his enterprise with an ability very extraordinary in so young a man. Not feeling himself ready to come upon the Parisian stage, he had organized a series of lectures in some of the localities adjoining Paris. He had arranged now with the municipalities, now with the literary clubs of the place. He had created a little stir.

One of the centres in which he had practised was that pleasant city of Sceaux, that Balzac has immortalized by laying there the scene of one of his prettiest stories. He represented to me, with much vivacity, the interest there was in sustaining his enterprise; he was all aglow with hopes that seemed to me illusions. He was so pressing, and there was in his entreaties such an engaging air, that I surrendered. I have never known how to say no.

"Choose a theatrical subject," said he to me. Dumas had just achieved a grand success with—I don't remember which one of his pieces.

"Suppose we take Dumas?" I asked him.

"Dumas it is. But remember that you will have many young girls in your audience."

"Fear not; I'll not forget it."

I had a certain number of ideas personal to myself on the subject of Dumas's plays, and I rubbed my hands in advance, thinking that they would of themselves excite a lively curiosity, even though I did not succeed in presenting them in an attractive form. I prepared the lecture without troubling myself about the composition of the audience with which I should have to do. On the evening agreed upon I landed at Sceaux. Lapommeraye awaited me with some of the notables of the place, and the procession conducted me to the hall where I was to speak.

I entered. If I should live a hundred years I should not lose the recollection of that moment. As far as my sight, which is not long, extended, I saw stretch, rank upon rank, the rosy faces of young women and young girls, and among these gay and smiling countenances some grave heads of papas.

I was immediately conscious of a sensation that between the lecture that I brought and this audience, as frivolous as it was prejudiced, there was an absolute incompatibility; it was like a gust of cold air blown in my face. I trembled in all my limbs. I saw that I was lost. I was not sufficiently master of my calling to reverse the lecture at a stroke, and substitute another better suited to the public. There remained to me, doubtless, in order to escape the cruel necessity of filling that hour, the means that Alfred 'Assolant had chosen: "And I, gentlemen, I take the door." I thought of it. Oh! I protest I thought seriously of it. There is no torture comparable to that of speaking all alone from a chair when one knows that one has nothing good to say, and that the little one will be able to say will be said awry.

My Début as a Lecturer

It was a rout—it was a disaster. I was to see, alas! many more of them; but this was the first. And I could have torn my hair (I had some then) for having gone of my own free-will, without being forced to it, to seek the bitter chagrin of this disappointment and the shame of this defeat.

Poor Lapommeraye, who was as desperate as I, showed nothing of it, that he might not add to my affliction.

"No, no," he said to me, "it has not been so bad as you believe, and as you say. But! there is one place——"

"Leave me at peace with your 'place.' I know confoundedly well that I have been execrable throughout."

"Bah! the next time you will take your revenge."

"My revenge! You're laughing at me. Never! Do you hear? Never! I will never lecture again. It's absurd to bring on one's self such emotions as these!"

And returning home I pondered all night on my unhappy adventure. There must have been some Parisians in the village gathering at Sceaux; for the thing was done on a beautiful spring evening. I pictured them to myself chaffing me and my ambitions as a lecturer; I was furious against them and against myself—triple fool! I should have liked to pin them into a corner, and cry to them: "This is surely the first and last time I shall be so stupid. You'll never catch me at it again—no, never." I had forgotten this old proverb: "*Il ne faut pas dire: Fontaine, je ne boirai jamais de ton eau.*"

III.

AT THE ATHÉNÉE-COMIQUE

It was the last month of the year 1866. The Opera was as yet only a vast work-yard shut in by boards; the sumptuous quarter that surrounds it to-day had scarcely yet risen from the ground. The rumor spread through Paris that amid the rubbish of the Rue Scribe, then in course of construction, a kind of theatre was to be opened, destined by its proprietor to be at the same time a lecture-hall and a concert-hall.

It was reported that a rich banker, M. Bischoffsheim, the father of the one who built the Observatory at Nice, and won his election as Corresponding Member of the Academy of Sciences, had put this theatre at the disposition of a society which proposed to revive the institution of lecturing, and to organize there, under the direction of M. Pasdeloup, concerts of classical music, pledging itself to turn the receipts, if by chance there should be any, into the hands of Mme Lemonnier, directress of the Society for the Professional Education of Women.

Everything about this enterprise was gratuitous; M. Bischoffsheim had graciously declared to the members of the Society that he wished no other rent for his real estate than the pleasure of regular admission. The members of the Society, on their part, had said smilingly, through their president, that they resembled all stockholders, in the sense that they counted on obtaining large dividends, but that they resembled many others in that they should not receive any. This facile pleasantry had much success.

Reporting did not exist at that time as it is practised to-day. However, the novelty of the thing had piqued the curiosity of some journalists who went to visit the hall before its opening. It was very extraordinary, and the descriptions of it that were given in the papers amused all Paris.

As the theatre was wedged into a hotel, of which the first story was reserved for travellers, it was necessary, in order to keep it the proper height, to bury it in some sort in the depths below. From the street one entered on a level with the second floor, and had to descend by interminable stairs, the relations of which seemed very complicated, first to the first tier of boxes, then to the orchestra chairs. There was but one cry: "But it is a cellar!" And the Parisians, so long as this hall lasted—it became later

At the Athénée-Comique

l' Athénée-Comique—knew it only by this familiar appellation, "Bischoffsheim's cellar."

It was very charming this "cellar;" Cambon had decorated it with exquisite artistic taste. The stage, always too small for a theatre, was quite large enough for the lecturer's table, or even for four or five rows of music-stands. The lecture was finally fixed in a home of its own; the austere amphitheatre of the Sorbonne was marvellously appropriate to the grave lessons that must there be delivered to an audience of select young people, and the professors of the old University; this coquettish theatre harmonized better with one's idea of a lecture addressed to people of society. You could see in advance in these boxes, hung with red velvet, women in full dress; aristocratic hands were sure to trail along the railing of these gold-embossed balconies.

The inauguration ceremony was very brilliant; lecture and concert for that time only, for the programme of the organizers provided that three days should be exclusively reserved for speaking, the other four for music. I was present at that *séance;* I had been specially invited by Eugène Yung, one of my old schoolmates, publicist of the *Journal des Débats* who, in his character as Secretary of the Society, had been charged with the starting and direction of the enterprise. He opened the meeting with a very neat address, in which after having paid the musicians the tribute due to these brilliant collaborators, he betrayed a livelier taste for the lecture which was about to be acclimated among us. He spoke with infinite grace of style of what he expected of the new institution, which he compared to the Royal Institute of London.

"Distinguished men," said he, "who may wish to speak instead of writing, can seat themselves in this chair in the midst of this hall. Those who shall have made great discoveries, and may not have official chairs from which to announce them to the learned world, may come here. From time to time there arrives from the depths of Africa, or some other extremity of the universe, a traveller who, at peril of his life, through a thousand sufferings, has penetrated regions which the foot of a European had never trod. He has seen people with strange customs, professing the most singular beliefs: 'Come here, Monsieur,' we shall say to him, 'you will doubtless write the account of your explorations, but you will give us great pleasure in recounting them to us by word of mouth. And be assured, Monsieur, our memory will keep without difficulty the lasting impression of what we thus learn, of what we gather from your lips.'"

When the audience had dispersed, I went behind the scenes to grasp the hand of Eugène Yung, who was full of joy at his success, and to congratulate him. I could not refrain from expressing to him my anxiety as to the difficulty of recruiting lecturers.

"There will not arrive each week," I said to him, "a traveller from the depths of Africa; great inventors who know how to talk of their discoveries are very rare, and as for the distinguished people on whom you count, I believe they will principally distinguish themselves by refusing your offers. You will very soon have exhausted the stock of known lecturers.

"I shall find others," he answered, and as I ventured a gesture of doubt:

"You will see that I shall find others," he repeated with an air of allusion so direct and so transparent that I cried impetuously,

"Oh, no, no, not I; never, do you hear; never."

And I returned to the house repeating to myself the peremptory and definitive *never*. I had sworn; I was resolved to hold to my oath.

Five or six days afterward Eugène Yung entered my house. I ought to say that I expected his visit, and had prepared to defend myself, for I knew by experience that there wasn't in the world a man more difficult to hold out against. It was not only that he possessed very persuasive eloquence. Certainly, good reasons and delicate flatteries abounded on his lips; you felt yourself slowly enveloped by his logic, at once supple and strong, without being able precisely to tell at what point you were most seriously pressed. He had the charming, the irresistible gift of seduction. But what made him one of the rarest managers of men I have ever known was that he possessed a sixth sense, which warned him of the peculiar character of the person with whom he had to do, and opened to him what Virgil called *faciles aditus et mollia tempora fandi.*

In the same way he knew the public, by a subtle and delicate sense of unimaginable accuracy. He foresaw just the thing that would be the most pleasing to it, and for how long it would be pleased. It is due to these remarkable qualities, that all the enterprises to which he applied himself turned out well. He was an incomparable director of a Review. It was he who drew *La Revue Bleue* from the miserable condition in which it was vegetating, and who gently, without having the air of taking much pains, conducted it to the degree of prosperity in which we now see it. He excelled in ferreting out from the young writers those whose talent was suited to the taste of his readers; he indicated to them his subjects, he corrected them with discreet hand. He had a singular art of awakening the curiosity of the multitude as to the work with which he was occupied; he never practised obvious or noisy *réclame*, he never stooped to purchase notoriety—that too easy and vulgar process was repugnant to his artistic taste.

You remember what Figaro, an artist in intrigue, said: "To enter anyone's house by night, to trick a man of his treasure, and receive for it a hundred blows with a stick—nothing is more easy. A thousand dull scamps have done it, but to undertake a dangerous thing, and to carry it out well and escape peril, that is the refinement of skill."

These words came to me when I saw Eugène Yung at work. To have advertising by paying for it—a fine thing truly! He was more delicate; he played, like a billiard expert, only difficult shots. He enjoyed talking with *chroniqueurs* of every order, suggesting to them articles for which he gave the broad outlines, so to speak, into their hands. He had a miraculous knowledge of the keyboard of the Parisian press, and each key on which he lightly placed his finger gave the sound that he expected. He was a dilettante, a virtuoso of notoriety.

Everyone was surprised suddenly to see in the papers articles spring forth and bubble up about a question of which no one had thought the evening before. It was he who, wrapping himself in silence and mystery, had, without appearing to touch them, put in motion the press and the public.

I recall as if it were yesterday how he organized the lectures which Père Hyacinthe, become M. Loyson, gave at the Cirque d'Hiver, and secured a triumph for him. It was not an easy thing to fill that vast hall for an orator who was execrated by the Catholics and in great discredit with the freethinkers. The entire press took on at the same time, without noise or shock, a tone of sober emotion. Eugène Yung had had the skill to group around the former preacher of Notre Dame the most marked men in politics and literature. All the fine ladies came to see the sight—the success was enormous. The amusing thing about it was that Père Hyacinthe innocently attributed all the merit to himself. Eugène Yung had gently warned him that the curiosity of the public would not extend further than the third representation.

"I will guarantee you three houses," he said to him.

The excellent man would believe nothing of that; he said to himself that he should be quite as eloquent the fourth Sunday as the three others, and on that day he was the voice of one crying in the wilderness.

I have very often verified in Eugène Yung the justness of this instinct. He knew his Paris and he knew men. He took it into his head to make lectures given in the Rue Scribe take. I doubted not that he would succeed in this as in everything, but I had decided not to embark in that ship. She would assuredly arrive safe in port, but what gain to me if I fell into water!

I had been to hear the first lectures that initiated the series. The audience had frightened me. It was a very mixed audience, very composite, difficult to move because it had no points in common, either of ideas or of sensations. In the balcony and in the boxes were women very much dressed, some even in full dress, who came there to pass the time until the hour for the opera or a *salon;* in the orchestra and parterre some professors, some students, and a number of worthy citizens of all professions and without profession, for whom the theatre was too dear a pleasure. The café-concert had not yet swallowed up that *clientèle*.

How was one to please people of such diverse origin. Neither Taine nor Weiss succeeded perfectly in doing so. Heaven knows, however, with what authority and conviction the one, with what elegance and vivacity the other spoke!

They both gave excellent lectures which would have carried away an audience at the École des Beaux Arts, or at the Sorbonne. They were listened to, they were applauded, but it was evident no one was stirred to the soul. Neither of the two orators, although trained in the trade, had for a single instant gathered all hearts into his hand—held them attentive, excited, charmed. It seemed as though the public, in lending them an indifferent ear, were fulfilling a duty of social decorum. It was the fashion to spend one or two hours of the evening in the Rue Scribe; people went there as a matter of good form, yawning behind closed lips—interrupting their half-naps with little "ohs" of feigned satisfaction, as when a charade is given by amateurs in a parlor.

"And you," I cried, at Eugène Yung's approaches, "wish me to go before this bored and *blasé* audience to play a violin solo. I who do not know the violin? I have not even the excuse of Sostène in 'The Saltimbanques.' He had never tried. I have tried, to my cost, and have been hissed."

Eugène Yung let the storm pass over. He knew me by heart, having been an associate in the École Normale and later in journalism. He was not unaware that I am of an impetuous and headstrong temper, but that one can easily lead me with a little patience, for I am weak in will as I have already told you; I have never in my life been able to say no.

He showed me over and again how, day by day, this audience had gained in homogeneity, though it was still lacking; that it would be an interesting task for the lecturer to meet it and form it; that it was animated with the best intentions, and brought to these sessions a kindliness and a curiosity that I did not suspect. He sounded to me the advantages of conquering by words a world into which my *feuilletons* had not yet penetrated; he recited to me the names of illustrious men who had promised him their co-operation; shouldn't I be happy to find myself in such good company?

He flattered my polemic instincts, he told me that I could bring before this audience some of the quarrels that I had raised in the newspapers and gain the battle a second time. He turned and re-turned me in a hundred ways, and I knew nothing to respond but, "No, it is not possible; I shall never dare—do not insist," and he insisted the more, for evidently I was weakening.

"Listen," said he, "try it at least once. You know whether I understand how to make up a house; very well, I will make yours for you."

"Ah! yes, I know them—these houses made up beforehand—these houses full of friends. They are the more terrible for those who fail."

"But no, I will give the hint to the ladies."

In brief he was so insinuating, so urgent, that I could not longer resist him. I made a gesture of acquiescence.

"I will, since you wish it."

"It is sworn?" he asked.

"It is sworn."

All that remained was to find a subject. The search was neither long nor difficult. It was a matter of course that I should talk about the theatre, since the theatre is the subject of my most usual meditations, and the most of my little renown has come to me from the studies I have made of it from week to week in *Le Temps*.

I had been working for a long time to gather together the elements of a theory of dramatic art, which I was always going to write and never have written. But is not happiness in this world the having in prospect a fine work which you can do and do not do, since the day that it is finished you will no longer care much for any one thing.

I had reflected a great deal on the subject of the conventions of the theatre, and I had a certain number of ideas concerning it that seemed to me to be sufficiently new. They are no longer so now, for I have put them into circulation, and every one has since taken them up to refute them or to confirm them by other arguments. Between ourselves, they were not new even then, for I found them later on where one finds all ideas believed to be new, in Aristotle. But, after all, I had thought them over for myself; I had given them the turn of my mind; I had imagined for them unforeseen applications to the plays of the time. It seemed to me that in setting them forth I should interest at least a part of this public, the part which prided itself upon philosophy.

"The conventions of the theatre," cried Eugène Yung; "admirable subject! You will be billed to-morrow, and you shall see what success you'll have!"

He pressed my hand with affection. When he had gone I fell back into all my terrors. I reproached myself for my weakness, I called myself a coward and an imbecile. But the wine was drawn. It was then that an extravagant, foolish, absurd idea came into my mind, an idea which makes me tremble still when I think of it, for it promised nothing less than to run my head into the black hole of an irreparable blunder, but which appeared to me most reasonable and the brightest idea in the world.

"What has been your aim?" said I to myself, "in accepting the risk of this lecture? It is to see if you have received from nature the gift of speaking. For without the gift in all art, one does nothing, one accomplishes nothing. If you learn your lecture by heart, or if you write it out and read it, or even if you prepare it too exactly, you may get applauded like your fellows, but you will learn nothing of the problem set you. The best way is not to think in advance of what you will say. You know the subject of which you are going to speak clear through; fix the order of the points upon which the development will hinge; but, the larger divisions of the lecture determined, rely for the rest on improvisation. If that works, you have the gift. If you get mixed up, you haven't it. The trial will be conclusive — you will not begin over again and they will let you alone.

This reasoning was most ridiculous. For even men who have, as old Boileau said, received the secret influence from heaven, whose star at birth has made them orators, even these feel, when they have a lecture to deliver, the need of long and thorough preparation.

M. Thiers, before bringing a discourse to the tribune, delivered it and redelivered it ten times — twenty times — before an audience of friends. Add to this that he had for a long time had a bent that way, and that he knew the trade. I had never exercised myself in the art of speech-making, and there I was pretending to hold forth on a phase of æsthetics without having thought out or arranged the developments with which I must surround it, without troubling myself as to the way in which I should present them to the public. It was a question of my staking my whole fortune on a game of *écarté*, and I discarded trumps. It was senseless.

Yes, it was senseless; but I gained this by it, that I passed the week before the lecture in wonderful tranquillity of mind. It seemed to me that it was someone else that was going to attempt this adventure, and I watched him do it, telling myself that he would probably break his neck; but, after all, it was much the same to me.

My heart only commenced seriously to beat on the morning of the great day. I was seized with an unrest that amounted to illness. Fear lashed me more furiously as the hour approached. I felt all the impertinence of my conduct, I saw the danger yawning under my eyes. I had scarcely touched breakfast that morning; it was impossible for me to eat anything in the evening—my stomach refused food, and every mouthful choked me. I was in a pitiable state. At home they begged me to send word that I was ill, that I had been seized with a sudden hoarseness. I rejected these propositions with horror. I held it a principle in journalism that the only excuse for not "doing" one's article was death on the previous evening. I considered a lecturer bound by the same obligations. When you are advertised you must go, cost what it may; one has no right to skulk. But with what ardor I wished that the gates of heaven would open and let down a frightful shower, or even that fortunate snow which had already saved me from a first defeat. But no, the night came on serene. I had resolved to go on foot to the theatre. The streets were full of people, and of each carriage that passed in the direction in which I bent my steps, I thought with trembling that there was perhaps behind those closed windows one of those before whom I should fall: *Ave Cæsar, morituri te salutant.*

The evening was divided between two lectures. Mine was the second on the programme. I had, then, a good hour to wait in the salon of the foyer, to which Eugène Yung had led me. I was so pale, so dejected, that he had thought all encouragement would be useless. He had, after some words about the kindly disposition manifested by the audience, left me alone to my reflections. They were very gloomy. I imagine that one condemned to death, about to be conducted to the guillotine, entertains sentiments not very different from those that agitated me. It was by turns an overwhelming depression, barren of thoughts like a whirling in void space, and, immediately after, a boiling of the blood and an anxiety that would not permit me to remain quiet. I drew out my watch every instant; let us end it soon for the love of heaven, I thought! It was intolerable torture.

I gathered all my forces to present a good coun-

At the Athénée-Comique

tenance when I was summoned, but I was so troubled that I made upon entering the most idiotic of mistakes. High up at the back of the stage, where the orator stations himself on lecture days, and which is occupied by the orchestra on the evenings of the concerts, there is an organ which is reached by a gallery. I have not very good eyes; I was very much agitated; I imagined, I know not why, that it was from this gallery that I was to speak. I ascended to it rapidly and I had no sooner made my appearance there than I heard from the dimly perceived distance a sound of an enormous burst of laughter. I stood confused, and instantly Yung, running after me, overtook me upon my perch and led me, laughing himself with all his might, to the table where the traditional glass of water awaited me.

Everyone writhed with laughter. Yung laughed as well; in faith the blunder was so funny that I began to laugh also. It was a farcical effect, and I was going to speak of the theatre. I drew from the incident a very gay exordium, and the laughter continued. Once started, all my fright disappeared as though by enchantment.

I knew very well what I wanted to say if I didn't know how I should say it, and what I wanted to say was worth the trouble of saying, I assure you. They were absolutely personal ideas that I could confirm by a crowd of facts borrowed from the current repertory of the theatre. Once embarked upon my demonstrations I forget entirely that I have an audience before me; it seems as though I am chatting with a friend. I put into it the heat and *verve* that I bring to ordinary conversation; I venture—or rather—no—I do not venture—the word is not a just one; all the familiarities of the most unconstrained intercourse flow naturally from my lips; when a word fails me I ask for it—it is blown to me from the audience; I return thanks, and they shout with laughter. I cannot complete a single phrase, but the audience does not care, it has the appearance of being enormously amused. It thought to see a lecturer, it had, as someone said, found a man.

A large man, with a good-natured face, with exuberant gestures, but without style, speaking with fine frankness, a little common in bearing and language, but so convinced—so impetuous! And then, confound it! there was another thing—I had something to say and I said something. The audience felt borne along on this torrent of badly chosen and incomplete phrases toward an idea that was just and (I insist upon this) novel, or at least unusual.

The success of this first lecture was, as happens in Paris with everything relating to the theatre, pro-

At the Athénée-Comique

digious, and out of all proportion to the reality. Yung fell into my arms in a transport:

"Well, was I right? You are ours. When shall the second one be?"

It was all hand-shakes and congratulations. As for me, I was as if stupefied and intoxicated. I seemed to walk in a dream.

I returned arm in arm with my friend Laurier, who was, as is known, one of the most brilliant lawyers in Paris.

"You've spoken," said he, "as a crow pulls nuts. It remains now to do with art what you have done unconsciously to-day; you have invented by chance — as three-quarters of the inventions are made—a style. You must make it your style. That will not be, perhaps, so easy as you think."

Ah, no! it wasn't easy; and I was not long in finding it out.

IV.

THE LECTURES AT THE ATHÉNÉE

In the first intoxication of my unhoped-for success I had consented to give a lecture every week. How was it that my turn could come round so often? Ah! the explanation is simple enough. Eugène Yung had to provide six lectures a week; as there were three evenings devoted to the lecture, and two lectures each evening. Now, lecturers were rare. The most illustrious among them upon whom he had believed he could count, had not obtained permission from a disturbed and jealous government to speak in this tribunal; thus Messrs. de Saint-Marc Girardin, Jules Simon, Laboulaye, Albert de Broglie, and Augustin Cochin found themselves refused permission to appear at the Athénée; others, members of the Institute, who had practically agreed to give lectures, had withdrawn upon learning the interdiction that had fallen upon their colleagues, and had not wished to avail themselves of a favor that would seem to be a privilege. I remember that one evening I was advertised with M. Léon Say, whose name had even been agreed to by those in power. But the subject chosen by him was not pleasing in high places. Notice was given him, at the moment of his stepping on the stage, to change it. M. Léon Say, instead of sulking over this ukase, received it with a pleasant smile, seated himself in the chair provided for him, recounted his mischance to his hearers with the utmost grace and wit, improvised a very pleasing exposition of the New Paris of M. Haussmann, and retired more warmly applauded than if he had delivered the lecture promised. These stories had none the less an unpleasant echo.

"Among the men of great reputation and of great talent upon whom we had counted," wrote Eugène Yung, two weeks after the opening, in the *Revue des Cours littéraires*, which has become the *Revue Bleue*, "many have put themselves upon their guard, since they have known what losses the list of lecturers has suffered, preferring to wait and see what names would replace those prohibited. Whatever may be the merit of the orators who have filled the void caused by this interdiction, it will be remarked that, the lecturers whom the Athénée has lost in spite of itself, were precisely of the number of those who were to have raised the new lectures to a high level at the very first, and given them a character such as would attract to them public attention and esteem. We were right, then, when we noted as one of the principal obstacles to the success of the lectures the ill-will of the authorities."

This voluntary or forced abstention of so many men of talent stood me in good part. I was only a *débutant* and offered only hopes. You know, or perhaps you do not know, what ardor thrills one after a first success. I no longer felt any doubts. It seemed to me that a crowd of subjects for lectures arose from the already considerable mass of my *feuilletons* and danced before my eyes. I caught them on the fly.

"Subjects!" said I to Yung, with the joy and infatuation of a *parvenu*, "I have enough of them to last till the judgment-day."

I did indeed have enough of them to last through some months of the winter at one a week. I hardly know of any exercise that has been more useful to me even in my trade as writer, than the one to which I gave myself up for that season with the extraordinary fervor of the neophyte. I proposed to myself to exhibit to the audience at the Athénée all my theoretic views upon the theatre. I was naturally obliged to disentangle them, and to render them clear to myself. I afterward tried them by the infallible touchstone of the audience, and I was obliged to reject some of them. It is needless to say that I do not wish to enter here into the details of the ideas emitted and the theories sustained by me; I only aim at recounting to you my impressions and the progress that I made day by day in this art, to me quite new.

You fancy, perhaps, that I gained assurance in proportion as I became familiar with the public. It was not so at all—quite the contrary. If you chat with dramatic artists concerning their *débuts*, all, or nearly all, will tell you that they commenced seriously to feel fear only when they were better able to measure the difficulties of their art. Without doubt one experiences the first time one appears upon the boards the particular sensation that actors have called the "*trac;*" but when one is young, one ignores the peril; one plunges on with unreflecting breakneck fury. It is like children who, by running, have crossed in a breath a narrow plank thrown from one to the other edge of a torrent's abyss, and who turn afterward and look, distracted with terror, upon the path they have followed, and say to themselves with pallor, "I can never cross that again."

I spoke every Thursday. With what emotion did I see the fatal day come round! All the week I had turned that unfortunate lecture in my mind, and as the hour approached for producing it before the public it brought chills of dread and terror that I still feel merely in thinking of it. I was tormented with all the anguish of uncertainty, never knowing whether I should succeed in mastering the audience, or whether I should fall flat.

There was no half-way with my temperament, which was aggravated by my inexperience; it was a smashing success or a tumble into a bottomless pit. And I could foresee nothing. Success or tumble depended—on what? I could not just say—on everything, and on nothing; on a first sentence coldly received; on a lady who rose to go out; on a chilly wind from the flies blowing unexpectedly across the back of the neck; on the least incident which, days that I was ill-disposed—days marked with a black pebble—sufficed to upset me and strike my brain with a sort of paralysis. I continued to speak, for there was no way of stopping or of fleeing; but I heard words reel off by themselves and fall from my lips independently of me, and it seemed to me that they had no sense, and I sweated with shame and pity watching them flow.

Those evenings I went back home despairing and furious. I went to bed and could not sleep. I have never understood better than on these occasions the force of the popular saying: *Son sang ne fait qu'un tour.* I felt indeed that my blood whirled through all my entire body with a sort of dull roar,

The Lectures at the Athénée

and beat impetuously in my arteries in great pulsations. Fever kept me awake until daylight. This abortive lecture rose from the depths of the dawn, and its developments presented themselves to my mind which worked then with a marvellous clearness. The words flowed abundantly, true and picturesque; it was thus it should have been said; where was my head? And it was precisely on those evenings of disaster that there were always auditors of mark in the hall, auditors who had been drawn by the noise of my budding reputation; what would they think of me? I had a foolish longing to cry to them, "This doesn't count! Come next Thursday."

I would rise from these sleepless nights horribly weary and heavy-eyed, my whole body as bruised as though I had received twenty blows from a cane, and I would set to work to prepare the next lecture.

"I do not understand you," said to me a woman of society, who did me the honor to interest herself in my attempts, "I do not understand how you can feel as you do. Lecturing brings you neither money, for you are paid nothing to speak of, nor glory, for no journal speaks of it unless sometimes to make fun of you. Supposing that you make a reputation for yourself of this order, where will it lead you, since it will never become acclimated in Paris? It is much time and labor lost!"

I felt the force of these reasons, but I had been gifted by nature with the tenacity of a bull-dog, which never lets go the prey that he has once seized in his terrible jaws. Failures irritated without discouraging me. I returned to the charge with all the more passion and energy. Nearly every week the *Revue des Cours* did me the honor, which it very rarely accorded to my colleagues, of giving an account of my lecture.

It was a young man, M. Léon Ferrier, now a distinguished professor in our University, whom Eugène Yung had charged with this duty. These analyses, written with infinite care by a judicious mind which knew how to let the light fall on the essential points, which discussed my ideas after reporting them, reanimated my ardor each time. I was enchanted to see myself so well understood, and often even disproven in so intelligent a fashion.

We did indeed have some fine evenings at the Athénée. I recall two, which at the time made their little *furore*. I had been led by I forget just which comedy of Molière, and as at this time I was being fed on Stendhal, I set forth the idea, which constantly recurs in the Racine and Shakespeare of the great romancer, that Molière had, in order to please Louis XIV., jeered at those who live by their intelligence and labor; that he had given them up to the ridicule of the court of the great king.

I had felt the moment I spoke thus a certain resistance in my audience. I persisted in going on, and suddenly casting aside the lecture prepared, I threw myself heart and soul into the development of this paradox. It was a great success, for when the whim took me I could have applied to myself what Perrin says of himself in "La Métromanie:"

"Il part de moi des traits, des éclairs, et des foudres."

I find in the report given by Ferrier an echo of this evening. The *chroniqueur* of the *Revue* spoke therein of the applause that I had roused. "It was provoked," he added, "by the familiar vivacity of his speech; by the abundance and ingenious turn of his ideas; by the curious and piquant recollections with which he sustained his arguments; by words that were even boldly and wittily profound; above all, by the warmth with which he expressed, à propos of his paradox, honest and sincere convictions. But——"

There was a *but;* there were indeed many of them. My colleague, M. Deschanel, was present at this lecture. Yung urged him to respond; he promised to do so the following week, and you can imagine what a crowd this oratorical tournament drew. I was beaten, first, because I was wrong at the foundation. I had let myself be carried away by the pleasure of astonishing and quelling a rebellious audience, and I had exposed myself in pushing to the farthest limit an idea which could only appear just if it were presented with all sorts of attenuations and corrections. Again, it was because M. Deschanel was one of the masters of lecturing. The session that day was most brilliant.

"What I cannot render," said Ferrier after having succinctly analyzed it, "is the courteous frankness that M. Deschanel brought to this discussion; it is that sure and supple speech, natural and elegant; it is that ease without affectation, that knowledge of his public, that wit always matched by good sense, that veiled archness of *bonhomie;* it is the art of bringing in happy citations which throw light and sparkle upon the subject; it is an animated and refined reading, that preserves the freshness of life in the masterpieces, and makes us see new intentions and shades even in Molière; it is, in fine, all the qualities that make M. Deschanel one of the lecturers most listened to and most enjoyed by the public."

There is not a word too much in this eulogy. There have been at the Athénée a large number of

The Lectures at the Athénée

lecturers whose merit I have not been able to appreciate, for in the evening I was generally called to the theatre by my functions as critic. But I have often had occasion to hear and to admire Deschanel.

He was charming, he was exquisite. From the first moment of his entrance on the stage he charmed the public; there was so much elegance in his bearing, such grace in his manner of bowing and seating himself. He slowly drew, with gentle nonchalance, pearl-gray gloves from his hands, which were small and dimpled; he stirred the sugar in his water with a dainty gesture; he threw over the audience a bright glance charged with sympathy. He commenced in a low voice, which rose little by little until it reached all ears.

Did he read? Did he recite? Did he improvise? I believe, indeed, that he employed in turn all three processes, which he knew how to mould into a harmonious whole. The sentence flowed without effort from his lips, always correct, sometimes embellished with metaphor, pointed from time to time with a shaft which he launched with a delicate smile, unless, indeed, he affected to disguise it by an air of indifference that made its intent only the clearer. He had a marvellous way of preparing for, and introducing, quotations, which gained in value from his clear and vibrating voice, his rich diction. He was in full possession of his trade, which he had learned at Brussels; there was such a certainty in his utterance that in listening to him the audience never felt uneasiness as to the result. They abandoned themselves to the pleasure of following speech so sure, so elegant, so harmonious; of seeing an even, steady light spread over the subject treated. When by chance the orator hazarded a digression, it was certain beforehand that he would not lose himself; that after having beaten the bushes and raised from them ingenious ideas and witty *mots*, he would return, by a detour known to himself, to his principal theme, where he would disport himself with gleeful and charming ease.

This manner formed a perfect contrast to mine. The difference, which was all to his advantage, lay in this, that he carried his to the furthest point of perfection of which it was capable; that he played upon it with the sure hand of an accomplished *virtuoso;* that he was a master: while, as for me, I was only a student still defective in the fingering of his instrument, and continually disconcerting the public by his incoherence and his defects of execution.

"You are insupportable," said to me the lady of whom I just now spoke. "You seem so little sure of yourself when you begin that one scarcely breathes;

The Lectures at the Athénée

one is afraid of some horrible break-down; one suffers from the discomfort with which you appear tormented."

With all that, I had my partisans, and I believe that I shall wound none of those who occupied in turn with us the tribune of the Athénée, in saying that of all the orators produced by Yung, Deschanel and myself were able to pique most keenly the curiosity of the public. Moreover, it must be noted that the others merely passed across the stage; Hément, Lapommeraye, Gasperini, and others never spoke with such assiduity as we. Their success was the success of an evening, and was rarely renewed. We two remained constantly in the breach.

Yung even proposed, upon the request of his public, to put us both on the bulletin for the same evening. We readily lent ourselves to that arrangement, for there was never a shadow of jealousy between us, and we always maintained a footing of good comradeship—deferential on my part, as I had been Deschanel's pupil at the Normal School, and held him a master in the art of lecturing; benevolent and amiable on the side of Deschanel, who felt, indeed, that my order of eloquence (pardon the word; I have no other at hand), with its familiarities and its somersaults, could only the better set off the sustained elegance of his own.

It was arranged between us that first one and then the other should begin. This produced a phenomenon that Eugène Yung had not foreseen, nor yet had we, and which was repeated too often to be attributed to chance alone. When one of us had in the first lecture a brilliant success, and had stirred the audience, the other who came after him found it ill-disposed and almost cross. It is very probable that the contrast between our two manners was too violent for the audience to pass easily from one to the other.

I never saw Deschanel upset but once; but then he was seriously so. I had spoken with spirit. He commenced, and, thanks to that sixth sense with which true orators and old comedians are gifted, soon felt that he did not have his audience in hand. He was vexed. It chanced that the temperature that day was low without, and the stage, owing to an accident to the heater, was insufficiently warmed.

"Heavens! gentlemen," said he, half-seriously, half-jestingly, "I protest that I am freezing. You see that my voice shows it. Will you permit me to wrap up my throat?"

He drew from his pocket a silk handkerchief, wound it about his throat, and continued to speak. But his irritation was plain. "'Pon honor, gentlemen," said he, smiling, "I am very sorry, and I

The Lectures at the Athénée

ask your pardon; but it is impossible to put two ideas together that have common-sense when I have cold feet. I am obliged to stop here and make you my apologies."

He gathered together his papers and his books and rose, without emotion or embarrassment, like a man of society taking leave of his hostess and her company. They laughed heartily and applauded. He had saved himself, most sensibly, from a misstep.

We should have asked Yung to separate us, but the season of lectures was drawing to a close; the inconvenience, if there were any, would not be of long duration, and it was imprudent to interrupt an acquired habit. The public, accustomed to see our two names on the bulletins, would perhaps cease to come if there were one only. Thus we went on to the end, and finished the campaign—a campaign that must needs be, and that was, unique.

Yung had been able to satisfy himself of the difficulty of the enterprise, and the increasing coolness of society toward it. I have told you that he was not a man to set his head against public opinion. He had expended, in order to carry this experiment through the year, much activity, address, and tact. He had saved his honor. He announced that M. Bischoffsheim took back his hall to make a theatre of it, and that neither lectures nor concerts would be resumed.

There was a widely spread belief at that time that the lecture could not live except in the shadow of the concert; that it ate up the money that the latter made. Nothing was more incorrect. The lectures brought in the receipts and filled the void made in the treasury by the concert. I had formerly in my possession the exact figures, which I have forgotten. But I find in the *Revue des Cours littéraires* a note signed by Eugène Yung himself, which is very significant. It was dated in the month of April, at the time when lectures and concerts were at their height:

"Is proof desired that the public is interested in the lectures, and that it commences to rank them with pleasures worth paying for? Let us take the financial side, the brutal fact, which is this: The lectures bring profit to the administration of the Athénée, and that cannot be said of the concerts. Yes, in spite of the care taken by those in authority to clip the wings of the lectures, hindering them from their true flight; in spite of the wrong done them by the erroneous opinion of society as to the pretended subordination of literature and science to music; in spite of all that, and in spite of the novelty of the enterprise, the lectures, sustained by the growing taste of the public, contribute to the prosperity of the Athénée, which, on the contrary, is compromised by the enormous expenses of the concerts."

I saw the institution disappear not without chagrin. I had taken a fancy to the lecture, I finished by liking the emotions which it gave me each week. Journalism was beginning to pall upon me; I had become almost indifferent to the praise or blame which the *feuilleton* brought me. I knew so well that of so great a number some must succeed and some fail:

"*Sunt mala; sunt quædam bona, sunt mediocria plura*,"

I could have said with Martial. And then, whether a newspaper article pleases or bores the public, one is not notified of it at once; one does not feel the instantaneous and burning sensation of it; while as for the lecture—the lecturer is the actor on the stage; he neither succeeds nor falls half-way; he comes out covered with bravos or is thrown over. There are emotions, painful, doubtless, because they are keen, but, after all, emotions; and emotions are—life. To do to-morrow what one has done the day before, what one is sure of always doing very well, or nearly well, that is fine progress truly. One might as well be a cog in an administrative wheel, at eighteen hundred francs a year. Nothing is amusing but struggle; to contend hand to hand with any chance whatsoever, to fell or be felled by it, is true happiness. The gamblers know it who sacrifice to this happiness their fortune, their health, and often their honor; the passion for politics, what is it for the most part but the need of struggle, and the need for strong emotion? That is why so many old men are in the Chamber, in the Senate, and everywhere, and are crazy over it; they have at their age no other way of giving themselves those charming thrills of hope and fear.

These thrills I regretted.

"Well, it is over," I said to myself when I learned of the closing of the Athénée. "It is a pity."

I did not suspect that I was going to reappear in a larger theatre, and take up with a wider *éclat* a new series of lectures.

V.

THE FIRST BALLANDE MATINÉE

At that time—I speak of the year of grace 1869—there were no Sunday matinées at the theatre, and no one imagined that there could be any. One morning there appeared before me the man who is entitled to the honor of having attempted the enterprise, and who brought the project to me in the first heat of its conception. It was M. Ballande. M. Ballande was at that time very little known to the public at large; it might even be said that he was not known at all. He had been, on leaving the Conservatory, engaged at the Comédie-Française to play there the heroes or the confidants of tragedy; had never been able to make himself a place there that he thought worthy of him, and was enrolled in Rachel's troupe when the great tragedienne organized her first tour through Europe and the two Americas.

He was not long in quarrelling with her. And when he was asked why Phèdre had parted from her Hippolyte, he had no scruple in relating the causes of their falling out. Mlle Rachel was jealous of him: when, after an act in which he had thrown the audience into transports, he was recalled with great shouts from an enthusiastic audience, Mlle Rachel saw with spite that when the two together reappeared to make their bows, all the applause, in place of going to Chimène, was addressed to the Cid. She could no longer support this crushing companionship; she had eliminated him from her troupe. She had often bitten her lips over it; for it was he who had given her precious suggestions for her *rôles*, and he knew from a trustworthy source that, many times, seeing the cold reception given her, she had cried: "Ah! if Ballande were here!" But Ballande was there no longer.

He recounted these things in a measured, gentle tone, with an air of quiet conviction, without giving the least evidence that he aspired to the presidency of the Republic. He was a cold Gascon, crafty and unctuous. Gray hair falling straight over his shoulders framed his broad and placid face. His movements were slow and majestic. Often he forgot himself and spoke of himself in the third person; it was a mark of deference that he owed to his talent.

This Gascon was a redoubtable man in conversation. When he commenced to elaborate an idea, the stream ran with the continuity of a tirade of tragic Alexandrians, and all hope had to be renounced

The First Ballande Matinée

of stopping or checking it. He was of the race of those from whom there is no escape, except by leaving in their hands the button by which they hold you.

I trembled at his aspect. I knew that he would give his ears to get back into the Comédie-Française, and that the Comédie-Française wished no more of him. He had more than once entertained me with the decadence of studies in tragedy in France; he did not leave me ignorant that he was the only artist in the world who could restore to the Rue Richelieu the cult of Corneille and of Racine. He had been Rachel's master; he would know how to form other tragediennes.

"*Et de David éteint rallumer le flambeau.*"

He pronounced it "*éteingt*," for he had the Southern accent, but so little of it, so little ! It was the clove of garlic in the leg of mutton. That touch of accent only heightened the flavor of his diction. Rachel had envied him it; but it was one of those qualities that cannot be acquired later at will. One must be caught young; must have been born in the land of truffles.

I settled myself to listen to the eulogy of the tragedy and the account of Rachel's last tour; he did not say "the great Rachel," nor simply

"Rachel;" he said "Mlle Rachel," with an emphasis in which there was a shade of paternal protection and of wounded sensitiveness; one could hear beneath it, "Mlle Rachel, who was my pupil, and who paid me for my pains with such black ingratitude."

But no; it was not to be a question this time of his contentions with the ingrate Rachel. He entered, grave, mysterious, collected, with the air of a bishop who, from the dais, gives the Holy Sacrament to the company of the faithful; he brought to me a project as great as the world, a project which he had long meditated upon and matured; a project which was going to revolutionize dramatic art, and in which he had need of my co-operation. I listened to this magnificent preamble with a certain anxiety. These Southerners are terrible people; one never knows with them if he has to do with a crank or with a practical joker.

"I have made an arrangement," said he, "with the director of the Gaîté: he rents me the theatre for Sunday afternoons through the winter, and I intend to invite the public to representations which I shall give of the masterpieces of classic tragedy."

I looked at him to see if he was not making fun of me. He was as serious as a pope.

"Pardon," I said to him, "but tragedy already

The First Ballande Matinée

draws but poorly at the Comédie-Française, even though it is played there with proper surroundings and by artists of talent. It is folly to hope that with a troupe picked up at hazard in the streets of Paris, on Sunday, between two and five, you will gather a crowd into a theatre dedicated to fairy shows, to see there the *Cid* or *Phèdre*."

He smiled benevolently. "I count," he said, "upon two innovations to attract the public. The first is a reduction of the price of seats; the orchestra and the balcony at forty sous, the first boxes at three francs, all the other seats at twenty sous; I wish to democratize art."

And he treated me to a superb tirade on the taste of the people for fine works.

"Let us pass on to the second," I said to him.

"It is precisely for the second that I come to claim your aid. I think of having the representation preceded by a lecture, in which the orator shall explain to this new public what is to be shown them, and put them *au courant* with what they should know in order fully to enjoy it."

This proposition would have nothing odd about it now. You must recall that time in order to comprehend how astonished I was. Classic drama transported to the Gaîté! On Sunday, by daylight! A lecture before the performance!

I saw myself speaking in a theatre, a showman for a magic lantern.

"Ah, well," I cried, "if you believe that by adding a lecture to a tragedy you have more chance of alluring the Parisians, you are very much out in your reckoning. Tragedy is not too much in favor, but the lecture is in full discredit. We have just made a trial of it. After a year of struggle Yung has been forced to renounce it, and his Athénée has become a theatre of vaudevilles and operettas. You will have two repellant forces, one upon the other. The lecture will put to flight those attracted by the tragedy, the tragedy will repel those who like the lecture, if there are any remaining. You will have no one."

Ballande was not one to be upset. He recalled to me the campaigns that I had so often conducted in journalism in favor of the great classic art, and above all, of tragedy; he held high before me the glory there would be in reinstating it, triumphant, in a large theatre, in initiating the young generation in the masterpieces of the past. If he had cast his eyes upon me, it was because I was the only one who was capable of this task—I, who was at the same time professor, journalist, and lecturer.

He understood nothing of my hesitation. He reproached me with it. In truth he spoke with much

The First Ballande Matinée

heat, and there was an air of sincerity in all that he said by which I could not but be touched at heart.

You must have noticed from these confidences in which I am so free about myself, that if I am very prompt in seeing the difficulties of things and in measuring the inconveniences, I am easily enough turned toward the opposite opinion if I am pressed with arguments that seem to me sound and solid.

"After all," I said to myself, "this devil of a man may indeed be right. At heart the French nation has in its blood respect and taste for tragedy; who knows if it is not, after all, awaiting an occasion to see it elsewhere than at the Odéon or the Comédie-Française, where it is the understood thing that it bores people."

The more Ballande saw me weaken, the more he pressed the sword into my side.

"Listen," I said to him, finally, "give me three or four days in which to reflect and consult. You have no need of an immediate response, since you will only open Sunday week."

He pressed my hand and took himself off, believing his cause gained. And in fact I felt at the outset a great leaning toward a trial of the enterprise.

"What do I risk," I thought within myself. "Suppose we do not succeed, and that is what we must expect, the undertaking will not be the less honorable. There is no shame in falling when the end one seeks is very noble. It will be a slight annoyance, it will not be anything grossly ridiculous."

I was nearly decided when I had the unhappy idea of speaking to my friends about it. Will you take a piece of advice, my readers? When you believe a thing good in itself, and you have any desire to do it, never consult anyone. One can predict with certainty that a general who assembles his council of war will not fight. I had for friends people of wit, Parisians; and the wit of Parisians, when they have it, is by preference sceptical, and, to cut it short, *blagueur*.

Every Tuesday in those days I had at breakfast from a dozen to twenty of them—sometimes more, sometimes fewer—who had chosen my little apartment in the Rue de La Tour-d'Auvergne as a place of rendezvous. We lived poorly enough there, but very gayly. There were a thousand foolish things said, and never a word of politics.

To this accomplished Areopagus I explained Ballande's proposition and asked their counsel. Among my *habitués* there was a clubman very well known in the clubs and on the turf. It was Mosselman, who is dead now. Mosselman was a fantasist, who piqued himself on knowing all circles of Parisian society, but who took pleasure only in those where people amused themselves. He was very well regarded in

The First Ballande Matinée

Parisian high life, thanks to his enormous fortune, to his illustrious relatives, thanks also to his caustic wit. None the less he haunted, quite like Hugues Leroux, the huts of the rag-pickers, and the booths of the mountebanks. I have touched glasses in his company with the Hercules of Neuilly.

It was Laurier who brought him to me one day, on Tuesday morning, to breakfast. As the house offered a constant procession of people of letters, artists, and actresses, he willingly came again. He was one of the most faithful, and we all liked him for the simplicity of his manners, and the humor of his conversation. He bore his millions amiably and gayly. We chaffed him on his immense property and on his race stables. When a new lady guest first took seat at my table, Mosselman was always presented to her as the millionaire of the house. She would regard him wide-eyed, and everyone would cry in chorus, "Ah! how beautiful is fortune."

I had hardly, at dessert, told my plight to my guests when Mosselman arose, seized a cane which was lying around in a corner of the dining-room, and drawing it along the wall, began in the voice of the man who exhibits a magic lantern:

"Gentlemen, you are going to behold Phèdre, the most amorous personage of the company. Phèdre, appear——."

An actress who happened to be there stood erect, shaking with laughter, and leaned close against the wall, gliding after the fashion of shadows which pass thrown upon the white screen.

"Admire, gentlemen," cried Mosselman, his face without expression. "She loves Hippolyte. Rise, Hippolyte."

He continued for some time in this tone, enamelling this improvised show with original sallies and absurd puns. We roared with laughter, I with the others.

The same day Ballande came for my reply.

"Decidedly no," I said, in a tone so emphatic that he could not but see that it was a final resolution, and there was no use in insisting. He seemed surprised and chagrined.

"Really," he said to me, "I had counted on you; I believed you had more spirit of initiative and courage."

The fact is I was none too pleased with myself. I had yielded solely to the fear of ridicule, and my conscience quietly, but keenly, reproached me. Why recoil before this risk—I who had run so many others? I did not recognize myself in this cowardice. But what would you? I saw again the tracing of Mosselman's cane upon the wall. I had in my ears the laughter which his exhibition had called forth.

The First Ballande Matinée

And I had, nevertheless, more than once sworn never to pay attention to this Parisian ridicule, which I knew to be the worst dissolvent of bold initiative. But one does not always keep the vows one makes to others; those to one's self are not to be kept more faithfully.

I tried to sweeten what bitterness my refusal must have for Ballande. I promised to announce his enterprise with a flourish of trumpets; I told him that doubtless he would not be obliged to give up the lecture; that he would find a less timorous man to take the floor on the opening day.

"Oh," he said, with superb confidence, "I am not troubled; I will have, cost what it may, a lecture, if I have to give it myself."

I looked at him with admiration. I was on the point of saying, "Well, no, I will give your lecture." I know not what shame restrained me. I pressed his hand with confusion. I heard an inner voice which reproached me with having committed a pusillanimous act.

It was the 17th of January, 1869, that that first representation was given. I had loyally announced it; I had heaped eulogy on both enterprise and impressario. I had tried my best to pique the curiosity of the public. I did not believe much in the great effect of this "puffing."

Le Cid had been announced. *Le Cid* had not been brought back to the stage by M. Perrin, in the brilliant fashion that is now known; when it was played at the Comédie-Française, on a summer evening, there were six hundred francs receipts. I doubted whether any one would come to see it, mounted as it now would be. Among the artists who had promised to play, some had taken fright like myself, and freed themselves at the last moment. Mlle Debay had been forced to learn in a week the *rôle* of Chimène, abandoned by the actress—half-way celebrated—who had accepted it at first. The Cid himself had fled at the last moment.

"So be it," Ballande had said, "I will play Rodrigue."

And between ourselves I imagine he was delighted with this accident; his secret ambition was to show to the Parisians, in one of the great tragic *rôles*, the master of Rachel, and to bury the dagger in the heart of the Comédie-Française.

Other artists had shown signs of withdrawing, it was such an unprecedented undertaking, one that appeared so extravagant, to give a representation in the afternoon—and above all, a representation of tragedy. Ballande remained firm. He alone—it was enough! The heavens themselves seemed to conspire against him; it was abominably cold that Sunday, and the

The First Ballande Matinée

rain fell by bucketfuls. "The unfortunate man will not have a cat," I said to myself as I went, more from duty than preference, to the Gaîté theatre.

I was very much surprised: the hall was nearly full—a very animated, and what appeared to be a very sympathetic crowd. The curtain rose on a spectacle with which my eyes have since become very much familiarized, but which was then entirely new: A table, surmounted by a glass of sweetened water, and behind that table a gentleman, erect, in a dress-coat.

Ballande had finally discovered a willing lecturer. It was an unfrocked priest, who besides, certainly had the air and face of one, M. Chavée, a learned linguist, deeply versed in the study of Sanskrit, who had given, I believe, some public lectures on the special subject of his studies. He is dead now: so I can say without fear of wounding him that he was more conversant with the Aryan language than with the theatre. He scarcely spoke of the Cid, which he seemed to know rather confusedly; it was more a sermon than a lecture. He spread wide his arms, leaned on the table as he would on the arm of a chair, quoted the fathers of the Church through his nose, and softened his voice where tremolos were called for. One could decently praise him only for the courage with which he had consented to introduce this novel institution; he wandered from the point, and was, frankly, execrable.

The performance was hardly better. I had never in my life heard Ballande, it was the old method in all its horror. He sing-songed the Cid, and always with that deuced accent!

Poor Debay, who was, after all, a charming woman, and in comedy an agreeable actress, had only taken a week in which to learn the *rôle* of *Chimène*.

"I fear that it is perceptible," she had said to me modestly.

Was it perceptible? Great heavens! Yes! It was perceptible!

And the others — what sticks they were! They had been clothed, doubtless, by the costumer on the corner, by contract. For Ballande looked after the economies.

There was a sense of haste and improvisation, and the prompter was very busy in his box. I met at this performance one of my old schoolmates, a fanatic like myself on the subject of the old repertory, and as I returned with him, "It is a dead and buried business," he said to me. This was not my opinion. I already knew too well the habit of the theatre-frequenting public to mistake certain signs which are perceptible only to people in the business. It was evident that all the defects of execution which had

The First Ballande Matinée

shocked intelligent and serious judges had not even been remarked by the crowd, troubled neither by the wretchedness of the decorations, nor the poverty of the costumes, nor the insufficiency of the actors, nor the dropped or halting lines.

It had brought a good will to this representation that was most significant. It listened to both lecture and tragedy with extraordinary attention; at certain moments even it had been transported, and the applause had broken forth on all sides.

It was Dumaine who had been charged with the *rôle* of *Don Diègue*. Dumaine, whose diction had always been open to ridicule, never spoke the Alexandrine over-correctly; but he had a magnificent self-confidence, a superb voice, sensibility and warmth. Hand-clapping and cheers greeted him; Maubant had never seen such an ovation.

It seemed as though all these people had never seen the Cid, and that they had discovered its beauties for the first time.

It was an entirely new public with which one had to do in these Sunday matinées. Collegians who were very much in the way on Sunday at home, between two and six, and whose relatives brought them there as a preparation for the baccalaureate; the *petits bourgeois*, smitten with respect for the old repertory, who were attracted by the moderate price;

workingmen seeking occasion to instruct themselves cheaply; studious young people consumed with love of the theatre, all that floating population who on a Sunday when the sun is hidden know not what to do with the afternoon, to them immeasurably long. The Catholic clergy, who are not stupid, had in the day of faith filled these long dominical hours with prayers and vesper chants. Vespers had disappeared from our customs and nothing had come to fill the void. "These will be our lay vespers," I said to myself. On the Monday following, in the paper, I launched the *mot*, which was repeated everywhere and had its vogue.

This new public was not very difficult, for all sorts of reasons; the first being that anything seemed to it better worth while than the weariness of staying at home; but there were many others. It brought to the theatre not the idea of seeing an amusing spectacle, but a firm resolution to be instructed. What do I say? To be edified, to commune in Corneille or in Racine; it never arrived, as it does in the evening, with full stomach, in the fever of digestion, sometimes heavy. It had that freedom and lightheartedness which is given by a healthy body. It was not, as it is at the Comédie-Française, or even at the Odéon, haunted by the remembrance of great artists who had made their mark in the classic rôles; it was

The First Ballande Matinée

not hindered in its expansions of curiosity or enthusiasm by the majesty of tradition, by the superstition of high art. It had felt a fresh impulse of admiration; it was *bon enfant*.

I took account in an instant of all these considerations, which had not struck me the evening before, and I felt a bitter regret that I had not attached my name to the first manifestation of this work, for which I saw a long and brilliant future. I proved once more the truth of the maxim that one does nothing in the world with that "good sense" which doubts or which mocks, and that there is nothing but faith for moving mountains.

Ballande had put aside every timid motive, however reasonable to ordinary logic. He had believed, he had marched ahead; it was he who was found to be in the right. He had convicted the wise men of error. On the morrow of this session I saw Ballande, and extended my hand to him.

"Well," I said, "I am with you, whenever you wish. Would you have me deliver your second lecture?"

"I accept," he said, "and in return I promise you not to play again in my performances."

This Gascon was not without wit.

VI.

THE BALLANDE MATINÉES BEFORE 1870

So it was I who gave the second lecture at the Ballande matinées.

They played that day "Les Horaces" of Corneille. I have never forgotten that attempt, because the remembrance of it links itself in my memory with that of an incident which was for me food for long reflection. It was then 1869, and I do not know if you remember it, but the idea of universal peace was in great favor. The deputies of the opposition refused, amid the applause of the public, the credit asked for by Marshal Neil for the reorganization of our army; a league was formed of the Friends of Peace, which published pamphlets upon pamphlets in which war was cursed and given over to the execration of the nations; a journalist of much spirit had opened in a very wide-awake journal a department under this title, "The Gayeties of the Sabre," in which he rallied the military men on their mania for appearing in public with their arms, as if one ought ever to have need of arms in the era of peace, which we had just

The Ballande Matinées Before 1870

inaugurated. Peace was the mania of the moment—the French must always have one.

As I had to explain "Les Horaces" to an audience of collegians, I had shown them that when two nations are neighbors, and join each other at many points of their territories, they quite naturally in time of peace form, by way of marriage, alliances between families of different countries, which war rudely sunders if it suddenly breaks out.

"Thus," I said, "let us suppose a family of Alsace, the son of which should espouse a young girl born in the grand-duchy of Baden; Germany declares war against us——"

At this moment there was a sort of outburst of disapproval in the hall, and from the midst of this disturbance came several strident hisses. I paused in astonishment, comprehending nothing; a gentleman rose from the orchestra, and in a very animated tone,

"The supposition is infamous," he cried; "it is a want of patriotism."

The word gave me my chance; I turned toward the man and apostrophizing him directly, I told him what you would have told him in my place, that in case war broke out I was sure he would be the first to go to the front; that we should all go.

"Yes, all, all!"

And I continued. I had reconquered the audience. I should have had them all against me had I persisted in explaining my thought,—which was the simplest in the world,—if I had had the stupidity to give reasonable reasons. But it must be that I was born for eloquence, for there immediately mounted to my lips a phrase of pure foolishness, a sentimental foolishness which lifted the crowd of simple creatures off their feet.

The fact is, that on this vast stage, before this immense audience, I felt myself immediately more at ease than I had done in the more limited frame of the Athénée. The exuberance of my gestures, the movement of my entire person, the familiar audacity of my language, the outbursts of a naturally very sonorous voice, and of a diction naturally ample and vivid, harmonized better with those empty spaces, where I moved in perfect liberty before these twelve hundred heads turned toward me, which I swayed with my hands spread out before me over the railing. There remained to me of that frightful malady of the "*trac*," which had of old besieged and paralyzed me, only a slight number of symptoms, of which I did not rid myself until much later, and which even to this hour, after thirty years, reappear, like an old gout—the days *de grande première*.

At the moment when the curtain which separated me from the spectators rose, my mouth used instantly to become parched, and it was impossible for me to retain in it a particle of moisture, even by gulping down swallow upon swallow; my tongue became thick and heavy, and it was a most painful effort to move it. My voice mounted to my head, I heard it high and piercing as though it had been some other voice than mine; I was stupefied and disconcerted by this tone, which was strange to me. It seemed to me that the words, articulated with difficulty, reeled themselves off aside from my will, and I sought in vain to pick up the phrases that fled from me. It was a very unhappy state, which only lasted three or four minutes. I knew, through the confidences of my colleagues in lecturing, and of many dramatic artists, that the greater number had experienced the same distress. I know of no remedy; I tried everything. A physician had given me I don't know just what substance, that I must chew at the moment of going upon the stage, and which had the property of exciting the secretions. It was in vain that they were more abundant at the moment I was to appear before the public. The noise that the curtain made in rising was sufficient to dry them up. I tried learning my exordiums by heart, thinking that all trace of emotion would disappear, and I should be like Master Petit-Jean, sure of my commencement. But I had no memory, and my trouble was augmented by the efforts I made to recapture my poor phrases. I finally resigned myself to the three minutes of torture. How many times, as I was awaiting the moment to go upon the stage, comrades or friends seeing me preoccupied, anxious, nervous, have said to me in a tone of compassionate reproach:

"How is this? You, after so many years of success, you who are sure of your audience, get yourself into this condition; it isn't common-sense."

Heavens! yes, I was sure, or nearly so, of my audience; heavens! yes, I was without anxiety as to the final result, being perfectly prepared; but I knew that, come what would, I must cross those three frightful moments; and I went over it in anticipation. Habit only, and confidence in one's self, cure this fear. I know actors who, after thirty years of fame, coming upon the stage the day of a first performance, no longer find, as they say, a cent's worth of saliva, and speak with their voice in the air, which they have infinite trouble in bringing down to the chest. I once saw an artist, whom it is needless to name, interrupt himself in the midst of a long recitative, to go to a table where were placed for the requirements of the piece a carafe of water and two glasses, pour one out for himself and swallow it, and his throat once moistened, come down the stage and resume in his natural voice the passage that he had broken off. He would otherwise have been incapable of going on, so dry was his throat.

With Mlle Sarah Bernhardt "*le trac*" used to show itself by a symptom peculiar to herself; her teeth would shut violently together by a sort of unconscious contraction, and the words would no longer come from her lips, except hammered out with harsh sonorousness. She only found her natural voice again when she became mistress of her emotion. The evening of her *début* at the Comédie-Française, as it was for huge stakes that she played there, appearing for the first time before a public hostile to her, with a rôle which was not within her range, that of Mlle de Belle-Isle, she spoke through the three first acts in that metallic voice which issued as though ground between her teeth. The effect was disastrous. She has never been able entirely to rid herself of this *tic* which takes her on the days of her great struggles. She has had the wit to make of this defect a manner, and has used it, and has imposed it on the public, and you see that the parodists who imitate her in the burlesques always try to reproduce this hammering of sound, ground out between shut teeth, which had at one time been only a symptom of fear with her.

During the two theatrical seasons of 1869 and 1870

I made a very brilliant campaign at the Gaîté; the Ballande matinées were, like everything else, interrupted by the war, and were only resumed in 1872 with a new *éclat*. It was in that year and the three which followed that they had their most glorious period; but before retracing for you, at least in its general features, its interesting history, I must tell you what became of the lecture during the siege. It was, with public readings, one of the rare distractions of those funereal days. The theatres were closed, for there were no longer any troupes; the men were serving in the National Guard. At the advanced posts the women were caring for the wounded in the ambulances. And naturally there was little thought of laughter at that time, and no one had the heart for comedy. But it was easy to ask of an artist to recite a poem for an occasion, of a lecturer to treat a subject which would not clash too much with the preoccupations of the public.

In this way, at slight expense, a *soirée* was given for the benefit of the wounded. Some of these *soirées* were very interesting. Verses were read there in which Banville derided the Prussians, in which Manuel solemnized our sorrows and consoled us for our reverses; but it was especially Victor Hugo, and after him François Coppée, who contributed to these representations. How many times have I not heard during those *soirées* the celebrated piece, "*L'enfant avait reçu deux balles dans la tête*," or the famous piece of the "Châtiments," "*Il neigeait, il neigeait.*"

The lecture was nearly always on the programme. I had given many of them by that time, and on all sorts of subjects. For I was beginning to speak with great facility, and without long preparation. One only remains deeply graven on my memory, because it was the most terrible scrape of my life, and if I tell the story of it, it is that it may serve as a lesson to the young people studying this calling.

M. Pasdeloup conceived the idea of resuming, at the Cirque d'Hiver, in the daytime of a Sunday, his customary concerts of classical music, and as he feared that this diversion would hardly seem in harmony with our troubles and despair, he bethought himself, in order to correct whatever there might be too fashionable in this pleasure, to interpolate a lecture between the two parts of the concert. The lecture seemed to him to be funereal. He applied to a venerable ecclesiastic, whose name has escaped my memory, to open this series.

Picture to yourself, in this day and generation, a curé in his robes, standing erect in a *cirque*, delivering a sermon between a Mozart sonata and a Beethoven symphony; but there was no longer place in our souls for Parisian fooling. Everything was taken seriously, even tragically. The address of this worthy priest was very short; he told us in good strong terms that we must not persist in the idle contemplation of our misfortunes; that music was a relaxation in which we should renew our courage; that art lifted up one's heart and gave one premonitions of God.

Commonplaces, but spoken with much good feeling and force by a man evidently accustomed to speaking to crowds from the height of a pulpit in a great church. His voice was full of authority, and it rang with marvellous strength through the vast hall.

This little discourse was, under the circumstances, a kind of master-piece, so appropriate to the time and place. I was ravished by it, and when M. Pasdeloup came to ask me if I would be willing to give the second lecture, I accepted without reflection; when the other had so easily succeeded why should I not have the same success? I saw none of the difficulties of the enterprise. I engaged myself carelessly, and thought no more of it, so to speak, up to the eve of the Sunday when my turn would come to appear on the stage.

"Bah," said I to myself, "it is only a matter of twenty minutes' speaking. I can certainly get through that. I have done more difficult things."

The programme advertised Beethoven's Pastoral

Symphony. The Pastoral Symphony! Nothing more simple than to make it the theme of a little discussion which would be in place. The purpose of music is to excite sensations and evoke images. The Pastoral Symphony brought the country to us, that country of which we had been deprived for two months, poor besieged people, who no longer knew anything of it but the slopes of the fortifications bristling with bayonets. There was, indeed, the wherewithal to speak twenty minutes, or even an hour if necessary. I can see now the "argument" of a professor of rhetoric giving out to his class this subject to be treated of:

"*Exordiemini pingendo campos suburbanos, ubi horrent arma et strepit bellum.*"

The thing appeared to me so easy—so easy that I believed any preparation to be needless. I trusted myself to improvisation, as I had done at the time of my *début*. I did not reflect that in that day I had chosen for my subject a course of literature which I knew to the very bottom, to which I brought, in default of the habit of speech, personal ideas long meditated and matured. I came here with a commonplace in my pocket, a commonplace of rare stupidity, to which I was, moreover, very indifferent, and in the truth of which I did not more than half believe. I amounted to little as a lecturer except for the childlike impetuosity with which I exposed and sustained the ideas that were dear to me; a commonplace subject which demanded only a fine choice of brilliant words, of delicate allusions, of ingenious details, was not the one for me at all. I ought to have been able to see that, and consequently take my precautions. But blunders would never be made if everything were thought of, and I troubled myself about nothing.

I seem to see myself once more coming down the boulevards under the bright sunshine and directing my steps toward the Circus. I had been on guard at the fortifications, and instead of going home to resume the customary black coat, I had thought it a bright idea to keep on the military costume, vest and cap. It was one more blunder added to many others, but when one gets started—eh? I was in a mood to ignore them.

I went along confident and gay, my hands in my pockets like an old campaigner, whistling a little air: I was to speak of Beethoven, that was a sort of preparation. I arrived; the Circus was overrunning with spectators. From top to bottom, on all the benches, a black swarm of heads. I believe, indeed, that there were there gathered together and pressed close all the people in Paris who could afford to pay the hundred sous. Even the rings were crammed with auditors, standing up and pressed one against the other.

At the appointed moment Pasdeloup made me a sign and I mounted the stage, where the musicians had reserved a small space for me. At sight of me a long murmur ran through the crowd. It was my vest which had had its effect: a disastrous effect. I had not precisely the air of a warrior, and then, truly, for a lecture, in that solemn place, before that assembled multitude, this costume was out of place.

I felt it at once. There struck me in the face a sort of whiff of reprobation that warned me of the ridiculous disproportion between this odd fantastic vestment and what I had come to do. I don't know how it was, but an old vaudeville refrain crossed my mind, and while I sought the first words of my exordium I heard an inner voice singing in my ear,

"*En le voyant sous l'habit militaire,
J'ai vu tout d'suit, qu'il n'était pas soldat,
J'ai vu tout d'suit, qu'il n'était pas soldat.*"

I did not, however, lose countenance, and by an artifice, which had already succeeded with me more than once, taking my cue from the very cause of my embarrassment, I set myself to paint the savage aspect of the fortifications that I had just quitted, and the desolation of the fields perceived from the crest of the slope. But I have not, pen in hand, any talent for description; true and picturesque words fail me. Still less could I find them when I improvised. I became entangled in my painting, and I commenced to stumble seriously. A detail completed my confusion. I had been in the habit of speaking in a theatre, where the orator has his entire audience facing him and under his hand. At the Circus, by the very arrangement of the place, only a part of it could be seen, and one had to speak with his back to a good half of his auditors. It seemed to me that behind me I heard something like a murmur of disapprobation; I wished to turn, in order to look the monster in the face and conquer him. But I had no dexterity of movement; I executed this demi-turn with a deplorable awkwardness. I felt myself ridiculous, and I was so. I still went on, for once on the boards there was nothing else to do. I felt that I must play my rôle to the end; but I felt my voice go up to my head, and the words, which fell unconsciously from my lips seemed to me to have no sense. One of my friends, who listened to me from the foot of the stage, told me afterward that I had the vague, wild look of an idiot, or a person possessed, and he had some fear lest my mind were deranged.

As for me, I do not recall a word of that fatal lecture; the only *souvenir* of it that remains with

The Ballande Matinées Before 1870

me is that, not knowing how to finish, I declared at the end that the French would be always French, and concluded with the cry of "*Vive la République!*" which had only a distant connection with Beethoven's Pastoral Symphony.

Of all the defeats of that kind which I have met with, that one was, without contradiction, the most galling. Chance had brought together in that hall a crowd of people who had never heard me speak, but who, on the strength of my reputation, believed me to be in the first rank. It was a sad breakdown.

Ten years later I again ran across in society some people who had attended but one of my lectures, and that one in the Circus during the siege, and they complimented me on it.

"Ah, you said charming things about music; perfectly charming!"

I could have devoured them.

"Stop! I was absurd."

I had indeed been so, and I could have boxed my ears with a good will, for it was my fault, and my very great fault.

One draws from a fountain only the water that has been first poured into it. In the mind are found only the ideas and developments that one has been careful to store there in advance. It is in vain to turn on the tap of improvisation; if the fountain is empty only air will come from it.

By good fortune for my little reputation the journals, which were few in number and only appeared on a single sheet, hardly ever occupied themselves with the minor facts of Parisian life; they were entirely given up to the details of the siege and the polemics of the war. I don't believe there was a single one that bethought itself to relate my misadventure, and I had the weakness to be very glad of it.

VII.

THE BALLANDE MATINÉES AFTER 1870

THE war came to an end, then the Commune. That horrible nightmare finally vanished—then we commenced to live again. You remember that there was then in all minds a great movement in favor of instruction. The more or less just idea was diffused through the public that if we had been beaten it was by the Prussian Schoolmaster. The people then must be instructed, and everyone set himself at this duty with the somewhat disordered impatience that we carry into everything, we French, and especially we Parisians, with whom everything is a matter of fashion.

The lecture was naturally benefited by this new hobby. I could not tell you how many projects were formed at this propitious hour, all of which sprang "*d'un bon naturel*," as La Fontaine says, but which did not all have common-sense. One desired that in each mayoralty, on every Thursday and Sunday, a reader should come to read the finest passages of our literature and comment upon them to the children of the lower classes; another proposed to ask of the theatres one day a week on which should be explained the history of the masterpieces played there, when it should be shown that art ought to elevate the mind and make the heart healthy. And all these planners came to me fuming with their idea, and asking my assistance. Had I listened to them I should have gone from lecture to lecture. Some even proposed to me to take me into the provinces to evangelize the departments; it is true that these were the very shrewd manufacturers, who assured me a share in the receipts. They were good apostles who wished that I should take up the calling of apostle to their profit. Of all these undertakings, of which some were never even begun to be put into execution, of which others had only an ephemeral success, there is only one that I take pleasure in remembering, for I laughed heartily over it at the time.

We who lived under the Empire remember what was at that time the casino known under the name of the Casino-Cadet, because of its situation in the street of that name. It was a choregraphic establishment, where every night, and all the night, belles of the quarter gathered. There was dancing, there was drinking, there was worse yet. Naturally enough, on the morrow of the Commune the impresario of the Casino-Cadet had no notion of reopening its doors and reinstating the violins. We were all just then completely given over to ideas of social regeneration; we piqued ourselves on being serious, and the can-can was hardly serious. The hall remained empty and abandoned, a very fine hall with vast annexes.

To rescue this hall definitely from the dance and from immorality, to regenerate it, as we were regenerating ourselves, by instruction, and to conquer it for the lecture, what a dream, my friends, what a dream! This dream a worthy man, whose name it is unnecessary to mention here, had conceived in the innocence of his heart, and he came all hot and eager to explain his project to me. He had rented the hall on very easy conditions; there should be four lecturers of us, one for science, another for history, another for philosophy; for me he had reserved the literary part. We should each have a lecture a week, turn and turn about. The hall would easily contain fifteen hundred people. At twenty sous for the first places, and fifty centimes for the second, we should readily make our eight hundred francs a night. The cost of instalment and rent was to be paid first, the rest should be used to found other centres for lecturing, and remunerate richly certain orators whose names stood high, and who could not be obtained without a strong inducement. The first year would be a year of sacrifices, but afterward what fortune!

And we should have the joy—while making money—of contributing to the regeneration of our land.

The gentleman who appealed to me with such warmth and candor was one whom I could not decently refuse.

"Listen," I said to him, "I believe that you are indulging in many illusions, and the Casino-Cadet does not appear to me a place marvellously well chosen for a first experiment. But you think you need me. I am at your disposition. I will open your lectures at the Casino-Cadet since you desire it. After all, I have seen Ballande push through successfully an enterprise that appeared to me even more extravagant. Perhaps your view is correct. Take charge of the programmes, the announcements, all the details of administration. At the appointed hour I will be there, ready to mount the platform."

Accordingly I soon beheld the walls of the quarter covered with posters, in which were announced in enormous capitals the reopening of the Casino-Cadet, and lower down, in smaller letters of various character, that the Casino would henceforth be devoted to lectures. The names of the four lecturers were given on four lines, mine at the head.

When I arrived on the day appointed, the manager came to receive me, very busy and very excited. The hall was not yet ready; he hustled the workmen

The Ballande Matinées After 1870

and domestics who had not finished. "We shall be a little behindhand this evening. You can understand, the first day, but be reassured there will be a very fine house. The audience is already very numerous—many women in full dress. It will take—it will take; you will see. Meanwhile, should you like to walk up and down in one of our side-parlors; you will find only a few there—you will not be too put out—you will be able to think over your lecture at ease."

I let myself be conducted into a side-parlor. Five or six groups of women were walking there, lost in that immense steppe of waxed flooring. They were rather *décolletées*, and trailed trained robes of gaudy coloring. I caught here and there some scraps of conversation exchanged in an undertone.

"Ah there," said one, "aren't they going to begin to dance soon?"

"There are no musicians yet. They are always late; it is disgusting."

One of them remarked that the leader of the orchestra had been changed. They wondered who the new one might be. They planted themselves in front of one of the posters attached to the side-wall. They read my name.

"Is that the leader of the orchestra?"

"Gracious! It would seem so."

"Do you know him?"

None of them knew me. But one of them who had gone on reading cried with amazement,

"But it isn't a ball after all; there is to be a lecture!"

A lecture! They paused at first in consternation; it was a heavy blow. A lecture! What sort of an "animal" was that?

"Well, *zut* then," said the one who had read.

And they all filed out indignant. They had been cheated. I laughed till I cried. I had only half a house to listen to me. There was no one at the third lecture. All hope of sanctifying the Casino-Cadet had to be abandoned.

All these chimeras were shortly dissipated, and only the Ballande matinées profited by this state of the public mind, and took a new start toward success. I will return to them to recount their glory and their decadence.

While the theatre managers, on the morrow of the Commune, amid the still smoking ruins of the civil war, sought in alarm for what they could best offer the public, Ballande had no hesitation; he immediately reopened his matinées, and the crowd flocked to them. That fatal year of defeat and misery had opened such an abyss in the life of Paris that it seemed as though a century separated the last months

The Ballande Matinées After 1870

of the year 1871 from the month of June, 1870. A torrent of frightful events had rolled between the two dates. Ballande, without difficulty, across the division of the brinks rejoined the two ends of the new institution.

It responded to the need we felt to regenerate ourselves by means of instruction.

People felt a kind of shame in presenting themselves at the theatre solely to be amused there. But the moment a tragedy was to be heard, with a lecture added, all scruples were banished.

Ballande had had the wit to take the lead. The remembrance of the classic matinées of the past was still vibrating in all minds; there was then, so to speak, no interruption, and the "lay vespers" on the morrow of the Commune met with the same success they had obtained at the end of the Empire, indeed an even greater success, and one of which the recollection remains dazzling in our minds. Ballande for the moment was a great man; the Academy, upon the report of M. Jules Simon—thanks to the powerful intervention of the austere Guizot—accorded him a prize, and all the journals sounded his praise.

There is always on the streets of Paris a floating mass of artists without engagements, some of whom have talent and a future; all held out their hands to Ballande and begged him to give them opportunity to appear in the ancient repertory. He welcomed them graciously, and made them fine promises, which he did not always keep. Among the actors who were known and already in possession of a renown acquired in the theatres of melodrama or *genre* there were some who dreamed of getting into the Comédie-Française; what player is there whose secret ambition is not to make himself a place in the house of Molière! They also applied to Ballande; they implored him to give for them such or such a play of the olden time; M. Perrin would be invited to the performance and would not fail to propose an engagement immediately. Even at the Comédie-Française there were *pensionnaires* boiling over with the desire to play a fine rôle refused to them in that house: "Permit us," they said to Ballande, "to appear in it just once."

And Ballande listened to them all, filled with his importance, and smiling. He felt the grandeur of his mission, and he bore the weight of it with a confident and gentle serenity. He walked peacefully amid his glory, taking care, lest their eyes should be too much injured, to soften some of the rays that surrounded his forehead like an aureole.

Ah! he had some fine Sundays! I saw there Mme Laurent, who passionately desired to play *Clytemnestre* and *Agrippine*, to terminate her career

The Ballande Matinées After 1870

in the Rue Richelieu; I saw there the charming Mme Grivot, now dead, and dead without having realized her dream, which was to play *les ingénues comiques* at the "Comédie-Française," and resuscitate "La Fausse Agnès" of Destouches; I saw there that poor Duguéret, who had so much talent and who ruined her life, appear in the *Pauline* of "Polyeucte;" I saw there a crowd of artists, since become celebrated, make their *débuts* or try themselves in great rôles; thus Laroche, now *sociétaire* at the Comédie-Française, played *Néron* there; thus I saw in turn Talien, recently deceased, and that amiable Dica Petit, who after having made a success of the theatre of St. Petersburg, returned to die miserably in France of inflammation of the lungs, and Mme Lauriane, also vanished, and that brilliant Jeanne Samary who was later on to have such a bright career, too soon ended, alas! in the house of Molière, and Dupont-Vernon, now professor in the Conservatory, who in his last book, "Diseurs et Comédiens," has recalled in some lines full of emotion the memories of that hour of enthusiasm.

Sometimes even actors whose position was long since assured, and who had arrived at the height of their renown, took part in these performances for the pleasure of playing before a new public more sensitive and more expansive. I there saw Coquelin the elder in "Le Légataire;" Mme Arnoult-Plessy in "Tartufe;" Febvre, if I remember rightly, in "Le Barbier de Séville." Mme Arnoult-Plessy said to me: "It is a pleasure to play at these matinées; at the Théâtre-Français our audience is always airish and cold; but here, what freshness and what vivacity of impression! The audience can be felt trembling under one's hand—it is an exquisite joy."

How many times I was involved in the negotiations that preceded and prepared for these matinées!

As I gave the account of them in Monday's *feuilleton*, and as I was one of the most assiduous lecturers, it was to me, as a sort of obligatory go-between, that all the artists came who for one reason or another wished to appear. Ballande listened to me with an air of benevolent condescension, for he had a friendship for me, and treated me on an almost equal footing.

He consented to lay aside for me his aureole.

"I have," he told me, "already a hundred and eighty-four young people registered who offer me their services." You should have heard the unction with which he lingeringly pronounced that hundred and eighty-four. Why didn't he say at once two hundred, in round numbers? Tell me why at a fair things sell for nineteen sous and never for a franc! A hundred and eighty-four; that gives you the impression of sincere, honest precision. An exact

The Ballande Matinées After 1870

reckoning has been made; a hundred and eighty-four—not one more.

And we debated together, as if the destiny of Europe depended upon it, the timeliness of a rehearsal or of a *début*. You may not perhaps believe it, but it is the truth that Mlle Sarah Bernhardt had a passionate desire to play at the matinées of the Gaîté. She was at that time at the Odéon, and had not succeeded in forcing the doors of the Comédie-Française. She had excited against her so many hostilities, some very treacherous, others very clamorous, that M. Perrin, in spite of my entreaties, hesitated to engage her. I took it into my head to sweep away by one brilliant stroke this slow resistance. What interviews! What negotiations! For she was not—she least of all!—easy to deal with. At the last moment, everything being well arranged, everything agreed upon, the Directors of the Odéon, MM. Chilly and Duquesnel, refused to allow their *pensionnaire* to appear, even for one day, upon another stage. It was their right, there was nothing to do but yield. But Ballande could not help bearing a kind of grudge; he believed that Mlle Sarah Bernhardt, by one of those inconsequences already familiar to him, had broken the word she had pledged.

"That young woman," he said, in a dogmatic tone, "will never succeed."

He would have formed her as he had previously formed Rachel. For he did not fail to distribute right and left his advice and his teachings, which fell where they would without the asking. He gave suggestions to Mme Plessy or to Coquelin. It was very funny!

Since he had met with success, he conceived a new idea every month. One fine morning it occurred to him to celebrate Lamartine, another day, Alfred de Musset, and he had the most beautiful of their poems recited with great ceremony, the whole, be it understood, always preceded by a lecture. He took it into his head once to arrange a spectacle on Holy Thursday, with the funeral oration of the Prince of Condé, which Dupont-Vernon recited from beginning to end without flinching. I delivered Bossuet's eulogium. Oh! it was an austere *fête*, and I assure you there wasn't the least little word to laugh at! But what will you have! People did even better than regenerate themselves at that time—they were edified. The public flocked to these communions.

One year it occurred to him to celebrate a jubilee of Molière's. He rented a hall, in which he brought together all the pictures he could procure of the great man, all the *bibelots* that had belonged to him, all the editions that had been published of his works, and, of course, lectures to explain these marvels.

He did better—he instituted a competition in tragedy; the prize of the competition was to be the right of two representations at the Sunday matinées; he named a committee, with the provision (this clause was expressly mentioned) that they should take no account of the frivolous tastes of the public. As the piece chosen was to be given but twice, there was no need to humor the crowd or to take the receipts into consideration. The project had not a shadow of common sense, but that devil of a man sailed before the wind; everything succeeded with him.

His committee put their hand upon a work, very incomplete, no doubt, but admirable in places, "Ulm, le Parricide," by M. Parodi, in which occurred one of the most novel, the strongest and most pathetic situations of the contemporaneous theatre. "Ulm, le Parricide," was played, and again it was I who gave the lecture. The drama, although it was written in very rough verse, had the luck to attract the attention of M. Perrin, and the author was not long in being admitted to the Comédie-Française with a new tragedy, "Rome Vaincue," in which Mlle Sarah Bernhardt, in the rôle of the blind girl, achieved one of the purest and most beautiful triumphs of her life.

Of artists and plays M. Ballande had then as many as he wished, even more than he wished. He also found lecturers, but not so easily. I presented some to him, as La Pommeraye, whom he did not yet know, and Albert Delpit, who has perhaps forgotten that he spoke, and with success, at these matinées. Others were suggested to him by the name they had won in that kind of exercise, as Deschanel, who was very willing to lend to three or four of these performances the *éclat* of his speech, also M. Legouvé. . . .

I pause at this name, for M. Legouvé was one of the masters of lecturing. It was the taste that I had, like himself, for this delicate and charming art that gained for me the honor of further intimacy with him. I heard him more than once. He had a manner of his own, thoroughly his own, which he carried to the highest point of perfection, and which I admired with all my heart, while quite comprehending the impossibility of appropriating to myself a single one of its processes.

M. Ernest Legouvé left nothing to improvisation. He wrote his lecture from beginning to end with infinite care, and this first labor over, he begged his wife, his daughter, or some of his friends to listen to a reading of it. Having thus composed for himself an audience, he studied the expression of his kindly hearers. Any development that appeared to fatigue them, every piquant phrase at which they did not smile, was pitilessly cut out. "What is suppressed is never hissed," said Scribe. He listened to all observations; one passage was not clear enough, another would be improved by abridgment, and he set himself again at his task.

M. Legouvé was, before everything else, a dramatic author. He had instinct and taste for theatrical effect. Read every book that he has written. Everything turns to a scene in comedy, recitals are changed into dialogues, and the theatrical phrase, the phrase that should catch attention, always comes at just the right place. He thought of the lecture as a kind of *vaudeville* or drama, in which the idea explained in the exordium as in a first act, is developed by a regular movement through the episodic scenes, anecdotes or digressions produced on the way, and carried the mind along by a certain though insensible progress to the *dénouement*. He excelled in those skilful compositions in which the expert hand of the man of the theatre betrayed itself.

When he had once well fixed, in concert with his family, the composition of the lecture, and possessed the written text of it *ne varietur*, he gave himself up to another labor not less painstaking, he applied himself to its delivery. M. Legouvé, as you doubtless know, for he has published some excellent books on the art of diction, is one of the best speakers of our time. He unites in this art two qualities that seem to exclude one another. He is both a comedian to his fingers' ends, and a man of the world, or, if you like better, *honnête homme* from heart to soul and from head to foot. Hear him relate an anecdote: he has niceties of delivery, pauses, emphasis, variations of voice which are almost disquieting by the ideal perfection that they attain—one dreads discovering in them a professional flavor, and a profession that savors ever so little of that of the strolling player. But these devices are concealed under such a brave and fine air of irreproachable simplicity, the speaker appears to be so disinterested as to the art that he unconsciously employs, that all suspicion of affectation vanishes; there remains only the delicious pleasure of listening in a salon to a gentleman of good society, who, being placed at the piano, plays like Rubinstein without appearing either to suspect it or be puffed up by it.

M. Legouvé attained by means of art the most exquisite naturalness. The least intonations were long studied, and I am sure that the most difficult thing for him was precisely to bring them to the easy tone of running conversation, to make their refinement always felt without ever accentuating it. It was by learning to speak the text that he committed it to memory. Then for the last time he got together his areopagus, he recited the lecture again, and only hazarded it before the public at large after a final approval.

And still he would not venture until after **he had taken** every precaution. He took account of the acoustics of the hall, **fixed** the place where the table should be put, sent in advance the arm-chair in which he was to sit, for he feared that, in a chair of **which the** handling was not familiar to him his movements might lose something of their ease. Do not **smile; only at this price is** absolute perfection attained.

M. **Legouvé** gave us only a small number of lectures—all were *chefs-d'œuvre*. They were masterly *morceaux* **rendered** by a faultless virtuoso. **I** remember one day M. Legouvé, meeting me in the **green-**room as he was about to go on the stage, said to me, **in a** half-serious, half-bantering tone :

"Why are you here? You **have** already heard this **lecture twice."**

"Ah!" I answered him, "I would have gone ten **times** to hear the 'Carnival of Venice' played by Paganini."

He smiled ; that might be at once praise and criticism, **and perhaps in my** thought it was both. I studied with the curiosity of a man of the profession that marvellous art of composition, that constant skill in the setting, that imperturbable science of diction, while the audience gave itself up without reserve to the pleasure of listening to such easy and such piquant speech.

I shall doubtless astonish my readers in telling them that we had among our lecturers Paul Féval, the celebrated romancer of former times, whose name was commencing to sink into the shade. I was his co-worker on the *XIXe Siècle;* he confided to me the desire he had to speak for Ballande. I was a little surprised, for he had never tried it, and he was near the age when one does not easily learn a new trade. But he was too important a man for his proposition to be put aside with a refusal. Ballande was enchanted to have his name on the bills.

I went to hear him. You cannot imagine his success! There was never anything like it. I was then able for the first time to estimate the fascination that eloquence and external charm have upon the crowd. Paul Féval had an agreeable person, a gentle, mystical face, with a habit of leaning his head slightly on one side as if it bent under the weight of internal suffering; he was captivating at first sight by that air of lassitude under which was felt, nevertheless, the Breton's solidly built strength; he smiled with half-closed eyes, an ecstatic smile which played about his lips, he remained thus for several moments, his mind occupied with some celestial vision. Then

The Ballande Matinées After 1870

his eyes opened; the hall seemed illumined by them, he had resumed possession of himself; it could be perceived that there was in the glance and in the smile a sly humor which was amusing by contrast. He commenced to speak—it was the most enchanting voice that I ever heard, not even excepting that of M. Larroumet, the eloquent Director of the Beaux Arts. A music of penetrating sweetness, seraphic music, shaded with the finest, the tenderest, the most delicate inflections. It was impossible to think of the ideas he expressed, one was under a charm.

Ideas! Great Heavens! he didn't express many and he didn't take much care to arrange them in good order. I recall that he spoke the first time on the "Barbier de Séville." He made, like the veritable romancer that he was, a portrait of that rogue of a *Figaro*, but a portrait so aptly dressed out that the audience nearly died of laughing. I still hear the little cries of pleasure that the women gave. I should have great trouble in remembering the rest.

I saw him from time to time draw from his pocket a paper at which he glanced. After the lecture, as I was in the habit of giving an account of them in the *XIXe Siècle*, I went to ask him for his notes to aid my memory. For there is nothing so difficult as to recall exactly a discourse delivered without plan and at hazard.

"Here they are," he said to me, "but they won't tell you anything."

I saw with astonishment on reading them that these notes were composed of the first words introducing each paragraph. He had written his lecture and learned it by heart, and as he was not sure of his memory, he had written down on a paper, at each stopping-place, the first words of the next passage, which put the rest in swing.

But afterward we had more than once occasion to discuss this lecture. He avowed to me that he had worked three months on it. "It has brought me in a hundred francs," he said to me, smiling, "it cost me ten thousand."

It was evident that at this price he would not give many. The fact is that he spoke only four Sundays, repeating each of his lectures twice in succession. But of all those who were associated with Ballande he, perhaps, took firmest hold of his audience, moved and charmed it most. I have seen women half-fainting; the effect he produced smacked of hysteria.

M. Hippolyte Maze, who has just died, a senator, was one of the lecturers whom I presented to Ballande. It was during the first period of the matinées under the Empire. Maze, who belonged at that time to the University, spoke to me of his desire to occupy our chair. I knew him to be already

The Ballande Matinées After 1870

deeply absorbed in the opposition, of an ardent temperament and impetuous speech.

"We are bound in honor," I told him, "never to speak of politics. We have to do with a public that is very sensitive on that subject. To pronounce in a certain way the one word Liberty in its presence is enough to make it thrill and clap its hands. This is easy success and we must deny it to ourselves. We only live by the tolerance of the Government. On the day after a scandal there would be suppression, pure and simple, of the lectures, Ballande would be ruined and the institution lost."

Maze assured me laughingly that my fears were chimerical, he would know perfectly well how to be moderate, even to abstain entirely, that he saw in the Gaîté lectures only a chance to practise the art of public speaking which he counted on exercising later.

"On this footing," I said to him, "I will try hard to get Ballande to take you."

Ballande, who, later on, had more lecturers than he wanted, was at that time obliged to seek them everywhere. He welcomed Maze with open arms, and I warned him to remind his new orator of the little lesson that I had given him. He did not fail to do so.

I could not be present at the lecture that Sunday,

but on the following morning I saw Ballande come in, not upset, for Ballande would no more descend from his calm than a bronze statue from its pedestal; but grave and anxious.

"Didn't things go well yesterday?" I asked him.

"Very well. A prodigious success, he has really most captivating eloquence. But would you believe it? He was to speak of "Phèdre," a subject that does not lend itself to political allusions. What did he do but take it into his head to say of Theseus, who seeks truth which is hidden from him, that it is the destiny of kings never to know the truth, to have about them only flatterers who conceal it from them, never to listen to the great voice of the people. It seemed as if the roof would fall with the applause. If there was yesterday in that crowd a censor or some friend of the ministry we are done for."

We were more scared than hurt. Ballande contented himself with postponing Maze, and when after the Commune the lectures were taken up again Maze had no longer need of this spring-board; he could launch himself openly into active and militant politics, where he made rapid progress.

Some of our professors of rhetoric in Paris, and notably Gidel and Talbot, also gave very acceptable lectures, but the heaviest duty fell, as long as the institution endured, upon two men, who were always in

The Ballande Matinées After 1870

the breach, ready to stop all the gaps, namely, Lapommeraye and myself. It is time for me to come to that. It was I who presented to Ballande Henry de Lapommeraye, who commenced to be spoken of both as writer and lecturer. He conquered the audience of the matinées at the first stroke, and held it as long as they lasted. No one ever had the gift of more prompt and easy, I might almost say fluid, speech. There was about him something of the lawyer of the court of assizes and the parish preacher. He was ready upon every subject, and treated commonplaces with extraordinary abundance of improvisation; that was the lawyer's part. From the bar he brought the gift of true or feigned emotion. He became tender or indignant, he protested, while he beat the air with his arms or struck his chest. His voice, which was very beautiful and very soft, was either tremulous with suppressed tears or broke into hearty accents. It had by turns pathetic tremolo or superb vibration. Leaning upon the table, above which he towered by the height of his great stature, he gazed at and fascinated his audience with his great wide-open eyes, save when he stirred it and made it quiver by a passionate movement of his black mane falling straight and long upon his neck, an ever-rebellious lock of which he tossed back with a powerful gesture of the head. From time to time he became genial, and with a gracious air, with a smile full of unction, he dealt out some flattering compliment to the ladies, as if he had interrupted a chat to offer them bonbons in a golden dish, or else he launched mischievously but without a suggestion of bitterness some innocent epigram upon opinions that he knew to be distasteful to them. They thrilled with pleasure, and whispered to one another, "He is charming, he is delicious!" The men were the same — he left them penetrated with the communicative heat of that always active eloquence.

What the orator said was not always of startling novelty, but he had the appearance of being so sincerely, so profoundly, so ardently convinced; he set himself at convincing others with such fervor of passion that they were moved, carried away in spite of themselves. He took possession of the crowd as Lachaud did formerly of his dozen jurors; he knew all the ways to master them and keep them under control. The artifice was at times too obvious for the fastidious. I have never seen the audience resist, or even make a show of defending itself. Lapommeraye in his long career as lecturer scored only successes. Before long we became the two columns of the temple of Israel. It was upon us that the matinées rested. Whenever a lecturer failed to keep his word with Ballande, or when the latter could not

The Ballande Matinées After 1870

find one to treat a subject that seemed unattractive, he sought Lapommeraye or myself. We always responded "Present," and went gaily to the front. The public and the papers associated our two names with Ballande's enterprise.

When the caricaturists of the theatre put a lecturer upon the stage, it was always on Lapommeraye or me that the actor based his make up, copying our peculiarities and exaggerating them.

I remember one of these burlesques which amused the *tout-Paris* of that time.

The subject was the theatres. Each of the plays acted during the year passed, according to custom, under the eyes of an accomplice who asked for explanations. Explanations! And instantly the lecturer sprang into view carrying his table and his chair. He seated himself gravely.

"I am going to give you," said he, "some explanations." And he stirred the sugar in his glass, and drank, and in place of putting the glass on the table he tipped it over himself, and dried himself off with his handkerchief.

"Explanations," he began again, "there they are."

And the accomplice grew impatient and ended by chasing him away. At the third appearance that the lecturer made, carrying his explanations, there was a wild laugh through the hall, and when the accomplice, throwing himself upon his table, seized his hands, crying to him:

"Do not come back! You are a bore with your lectures," they writhed and collapsed with laughter. All eyes were turned toward me, and I laughed with all my heart, for it was I that the Aristophanes of the burlesque had caricatured in that scene. Lapommeraye had his turn the following year, and Saint-Germain made a very similar attack upon him, which was almost too near the truth to be truly comical, for the model must not be too exactly copied in this kind of caricature. Only the most salient features should be taken and enlarged upon with a proper feeling for the grotesque. For that matter we both lent ourselves to caricature, for we both had very obvious processes and mannerisms easy to catch and push to absurdity.

I am sure that during these few years of vogue I reviewed all the classic masterpieces, and moreover, a considerable number of works of the second order which Ballande exhumed on the score of curiosity. For instance, he gave the "Phèdre" of Pradon, "La Fausse Agnès" by Destouches, "Le Martyr de Saint-Genest" of Rotrou; he tried once to render one of Racine's tragedies with the *mise en scène* of the period. He had placed at the sides of the stage three rows of benches, on which he had seated some supernumeraries who represented the courtiers of the great king. They represented them, alas! in the shabbiest way—the wretches looked as if they were being bored at forty cents an hour. Were they even paid that much indeed? I was charged with presenting them to the audience, and relating to it the revolution that Voltaire made in the eighteenth century, when he freed the stage and chased away the crowd of young lords who had for a long time encumbered it.

The lecturer had in these representations the largest part of the responsibility, and he also gained the most credit from them. I shall not tell you of the success that I may have attained in this direction. I shall only bring to mind the recollection of one or two matinées which influenced my life in an especial way.

I then wrote every morning for the *XIXe Siècle*, which all Paris read. I no longer know what folly it was that our students permitted themselves in one of the Paris colleges that led me to address a little lecture to them in that paper, and I made use in the course of the article of the epithet, *those mischievous monkeys.*

I attached no further importance to it, nor did About, who let the phrase pass. You know how hotheaded young people are; they took fire at this insult—they formed a company, a party was made to rent the orchestra of the theatre, and there hiss the insulter of French youth. I suspected nothing, when on Saturday morning I received a note from my old friend Maxime Gaucher, the same whose easy and refined criticisms have long been relished by the readers of the *Revue Bleue*. "I have," he wrote, "just captured in my class a list of subscriptions on which the names of the greater number of my pupils were inscribed. I interrogated one of them, who has revealed the horrible secret to me. They are organizing for Sunday a furious 'smoking out' for you. I have not even tried to dissuade them. You know yourself that no counsel would be listened to. We must let them go on, and laugh at it. I warn you so that you may not be taken unawares and disconcerted; keep on your guard."

In truth I only laughed at this warning. I was born with the instinct of combativeness. The expectation of a battle excites and amuses me.

I informed Ballande, who asked me if I didn't want him to take measures for the co-operation of the police: "Not for the world," I said to him, "I will get out of this business by myself; these are gamins; they promise themselves some fun. Don't let us spoil it for them; when they are tired of shouting I will take advantage of it and deliver the lecture."

That was also Ballande's opinion. At heart he was enchanted. Beyond the fact that the house was filled from top to bottom for this especial matinée, he foresaw that the noise of this manifestation would have its echo in the newspapers, the gift of a grand advertisement falling to him from heaven like gratuitous manna.

At noon, according to my habit, I set out on foot, pondering all along the streets and boulevards upon the beginning of my lecture. Just at the moment of entering the theatre by the artists' door I saw two persons detach themselves from a somewhat numerous group stationed on the sidewalk, and approach with the evident intention of speaking to me.

"Heavens! M. Sarcey," one of them said to me, "we are not known to you; but we are fathers of families, and we come to you in advance to make our apologies for our rascals of boys, who propose to make a great row for you. We have done all that we could to turn them from this project; but they are enraged. It only remains for us to ask your pardon. For the rest, we have ourselves taken seats, and we shall be there to sustain you."

"You remind me of **Brutus**," I said to him, laughing. I thanked these gentlemen for their kindness, pressed their hands, and entered.

There was a little nervousness in the side-scenes. The actors had got wind of what was going on. Artists as a rule don't like to have hissing come into the game in theatrical matters. It is not exactly interest or friendship for comrades; it is rather that when the public is once let loose it cares not for anyone or anything. You can never tell just where it will stop. It is the cat in the fable, who after having munched the neighbor's sparrow finds the flavor exquisite and devours others. I was perhaps the only one who kept his *sang-froid* and his good-humor. The idea of fathers and sons contending in my honor—*plus quam civilia bella*—made me cheerful.

I had no sooner pronounced the consecrated formula, "Mesdames, messieurs," than the storm broke. Ah, my friends! What a racket! They all had rattling whistles, and they interrupted their hissing only to shout; savage yells, the cries of various animals, and from time to time upon the air of the footlights: "Apologies! apologies!" Some fiercer ones even cried, "No apologies! Put him out!"

I waited, resigned and smiling. At the least sign of clearing I tried to throw in a phrase, which was instantly drowned by an enormous uproar. I did not insist. I economized my strength and my voice.

My tactics were to let the brawlers exhaust themselves. I was convinced that the real audience after being amused for ten or fifteen minutes by this disturbance would in the end tire of it, would take my part in a body and impose silence upon them.

This calculation, which was shrewd enough, found, by the merest chance, an auxiliary upon whom I had not counted. In the stage-box at the left there was, besides Ballande, a lawyer with whom I was slightly acquainted, for he was the brother of M. Laya, the author of the "Duc Job," that has just been revived at the Comédie-Française. He possessed an enormous voice, what we call a "good deep," an extraordinary flow of speech, and a still more extraordinary desire to employ both, cost what it might. He climbed over the ledge of the box, leapt upon the stage, pressed my hand, and shouted back across the tumult.

At this unexpected reinforcement the assailants redoubled their fury, there was a new tempest of cries and hisses. He stood his ground. I hear him singing my praises and those of Ballande, those of Racine, those of the matinées, those of the youth, of that noble youth who may doubtless be misled for an instant, but who can, by a word—a single word direct from the heart—be brought around to great thoughts and to generous sentiments.

He uttered many of them, which fell as they might, and the youth were not brought round. But they weakened sensibly; there only remained two groups of the ill-disposed, which formed two very distinct spots, one in the orchestra, the other in the high galleries. The isolated hissers were stifled either by weariness or because their neighbors had imposed silence upon them. The battalion of the fathers seized the moment.

"Now *we* rise!" as would soon be said in "Le Cid." Some voices cried:

"Put out the college rascals!"

"Let us hear!"

"It is absurd!"

"It is revolting!"

I saw an elderly man take one of these gamins by the ear. "Behave yourself, little scamp."

There was laughter; the audience decidedly rebelled; that was the moment my defender chose to set off again. I threw myself upon him. I begged him to let me alone. I pushed him gently toward the side-scenes. He struggled. He actually wished to offer me the assistance of a new discourse. I held out against it.

"He will go!"

"He will not go!"

He goes. He is gone. I return to the stage a victor.

"Mesdames, messieurs." A new volley of hisses, but this time the audience rises to its feet, furious.

The Ballande Matinées After 1870

"The police—the police! Are there no police in the theatre?"

They arrive in the shape of the municipal guard, and their uniforms appear in the third gallery. The most determined members of the cabal are indicated to them, they gather them in neatly, in spite of individual resistance, and lead them out of the house. The same performance is started in the orchestra, but the conspirators prefer to lay down their arms. They have the good grace to put their rattling whistles in their pockets, the insurrection is put down. Order reigns in Warsaw.

"Mesdames, messieurs, we have lost twenty-five minutes. I will try and make it up to you."

And with an extraordinary transport of speech I give a lecture. Oh! such a lecture! I have related some of my failures to you; it is the least I can do to tell you also of my days of triumph. That time I fully tasted the delicious pleasure of feeling an audience vibrate under my hand. As I was near the end a timid hiss came from a corner of the orchestra.

"Ah, my young friend," I said to him, "your watch is forty minutes behind time."

The phrase was not specially witty; but had it been a hundred times more stupid it would have been applauded just the same; there was an explosion of laughter and bravos. Upon leaving the hall I went, as you may imagine, to ask pardon for those who had been taken to the guard-house. I pressed their hands after a little paternal admonition. One of them, more arrogant than the others, said to me, shaking his head, that it couldn't end this way, and that I should be hissed yet. He used another word that I do not wish to write.

"Ah! well," I said, "my friend, I do not wish to deprive you of that little pleasure. I was not to speak next Sunday; but in order to please you I will beg Lapommeraye to grant me his turn in lecturing; be careful not to get kept in."

The report of these little incidents was noised abroad among the public, so that on the following Sunday the house was crammed; there were even people in the corridors. And behold of what success and failure consist in lecturing.

The audience was visibly preoccupied; it awaited a manifestation which did not come. As for me, I prepared (which was a blunder) some piquant phrases for which I could not find a place. I was uneasy. In the audience there was a certain reserve; I could not succeed in breaking that thin layer of ice. I spoke coldly, and they listened to me in the same way.

It is always a very delicate undertaking to give a lecture before an absent-minded audience. It takes

The Ballande Matinées After 1870

infinite pains to bring them over, sometimes one succeeds. I remember, à propos of this, a little story in which I played a part.

The organizers of a charity fête were given the Salle du Châtelet, and to force the receipts they had thought of applying to Edmond About. About was then in full enjoyment of his renown. No one was ignorant of the fact that he was a sparkling talker, and he had never spoken in public, which doubled the curiosity to hear him. When it was known that he had accepted, when his name shone on the posters it was as though Patti had been about to sing—in two days the immense Salle du Châtelet was rented from top to bottom. Tickets sold at a premium.

About had given his name a little imprudently. The noise it made, both in the papers and among the public, disquieted him beyond measure. There was in this art of talking with twelve hundred persons an enormous technical element that he had not learned. It would have been painful to him to attain only a *succès d'estime*. He did not feel sure of himself. The evening before we saw him come in at the *XIXe Siècle* office, his neck enveloped in a muffler, and speaking with difficulty.

"The deuce!" I said to him, "won't your voice work? How about to-morrow!"

"I will try to be in condition," he replied, and thereupon I left him.

The morrow was Sunday—the famous Sunday. At eight o'clock in the morning my bell rang, and one of the organizers of the fête entered, frightened, wild.

"Here, read that," he said, tendering me a letter. About sent him word that bronchitis confined him to his bed; he urged them to come to me, assuring them that I would get them out of the scrape. To this letter was added another, addressed to me personally. About begged me to keep his engagement, it was a service that he expected of my old friendship.

My first idea was to refuse plumply. Think of my going to speak—a poor provincial barytone—before a house which counted on Faure, which had paid to hear him, which would be horribly disappointed, and which would perhaps slip out, leaving me alone with my disgrace.

"The receipts must be saved," cried my man, in despair. "Enormous, frightful receipts; for the poor; it is to the poor that you sacrifice yourself. Come, consent! The public will be grateful to you for it."

"But the subject of the lecture is announced! I have nothing ready à propos of it, and there is no way of changing it, since you are to give the play afterward."

"Bah! it relates to the theatre—you are always ready on that subject."

While we were arguing another letter arrived, brought by About's servant.

He insisted forcibly upon the embarrassment that I should impose upon him and the worthy people who were placed at the head of this good work, if I did not accept.

"Very well! I surrender," I said.

They did not put a paster on the bill; they did not apprise the public of the change of scene. They were too much afraid of desertion in a body before my entrance on the stage. It was supposed that, the curtain once raised, the audience would reconcile themselves to the substitution, satisfied or not satisfied, of small matter: the essential thing was not to give back the money.

The curtain rises; I advance to the rail, moving my table as was my custom to the prompter's hole. While engaged in this operation I heard run from the top to the bottom of the hall a murmur of surprise and disappointment.

"Well! yes," I said, gazing at the audience, "it is only I," and I accompanied the phrase with a gesture of resignation and humility which was, it appears, so irresistibly comic that the entire house burst into laughter. This beginning encouraged me. I began to tell with much animation and good-humor about About's cold, the insistence of these gentlemen, my anxiety about the audience. I painted for them the state of mind that they had just passed through; everyone recognized the picture and they laughed still more heartily. I enter upon the chosen subject; from time to time I stop: " That is not what About would have said—would you like me to tell you what About would have said—and would have said much better, doubtless?" And I make him speak, and I respond to him; it is a comedy, the salt of which lay in the childish gayety of the improvisation. I have hardly had in my life as lecturer a more instantaneous and complete success. The next day I received from the organizers of the fête a monumental inkstand with this inscription: *Vale, scribe et ora;* it is in this inkstand that I dip my pen to-day to tell you this story.

Everything has an end in this world. It was the very success of the Ballande matinées that killed them. All the managers, seeing that to invite the public to come on Sunday afternoon brought in fine receipts, organized matinées in their theatres. They only came to it slowly, one after another, with great reluctance, but they came to it. There is not a place in the world where the spirit of routine has such narrowness, strength, and tenacity, as in the

The Ballande Matinées After 1870

theatre. It would seem to you, wouldn't it, that at the first rumor of the infatuation of the Parisian public for the Sunday matinées, all the managers, aroused, must have thrown themselves on this unexpected manna. Instead they hesitated a long time.

I was then on very pleasant terms with Montigny, the director of the Gymnase, who was, thank heaven! very intelligent and full of initiative. As soon as I saw the public crowding Ballande's house, I sought Montigny and represented to him with warmth that there would be much money gained for him, and it would be a service rendered to art if each Sunday he would give us in the afternoon some work of the old Théâtre de Madame, reproduced with care. I still see Montigny listening to me with an air of disdainful condescension, and saying to me in his cutting, autocratic voice, impatient of all contradiction:

"Performances in the daytime? It is senseless!"

He gave up, nevertheless, vanquished later on by example; but he never liked to dip his own hands in that business so subversive of all tradition. He put it upon Landrol, an excellent comedian, who steered it as best he could, far from the master's eye. The master pocketed the money, none the less, for these matinées brought him in a great deal; but he sighed and lamented to himself the decadence of the theatre.

As this movement became marked, poor Ballande saw the profits of his matinées decrease. It troubled him; he suffered from it; his grief gave me pain; nevertheless I can't think of it without laughing. How funny it was when he entered my study, majestic and irritated:

"Still another announcing matinées! The whole world is robbing me! I am being plundered! It is an outrage! Can the government permit me to be so despoiled?"

And, seriously, he consulted me upon the chances he would have in beginning a lawsuit against all the sharpers who had stolen his idea! He wrote petitions to the ministers to ask national compensation. I would almost venture to say that he solicited the direction of the Comédie-Française, and that he predicted an evil future when he learned that it had been given into other hands.

If he had been content to pour his complaints into my waistcoat, it would only have been half bad for him; but he spread them abroad, with an impartiality very rare in our iron age, upon all whom he met. He was in a fair way to become ridiculous.

He had always conducted his business with much economy, an economy which was imposed on him by the necessities of his work, but which also belonged to his temperament. He had had up to that time, at very small cost, the hall in which he gave his representations, and the actors who played for him for the honor of it, and I will even add his lecturers, for whom these matinées were a field for practice—a palestra. Now that there were matinées everywhere, he saw the necessity of raising his salaries, and nothing could affect him more dolefully. With his eyes upturned to heaven, he called upon it to witness the ingratitude of artists who asked of him a compensation of twenty francs. And he had trained them. He had given them counsel. They had resented it in the green-room. There is a crowd of legends about him, which by dint of repetition were taken for truth. How many times have I not heard an anecdote which always raised a laugh.

One day he had played Alceste in the "Misanthrope," and as he had lent it his accent and his jargon, he had been from the first act greatly guyed by an audience inclined to that sport. He entered the side-scenes, and cried with a scandalized air:

"Oh, my friends, this is the first time I ever heard Molière hissed. Poor France!"

Let us add that the public was little by little tiring of lectures. Besides the fact that all were not amusing, the number of subjects is not infinite, and the same ones appeared more than once on the bills.

I remember an irritated letter that I received one

day from an honorable inhabitant of the provinces, who, finding his way to Paris, had come to hear me speak of "Le Barbier de Séville."

"Monsieur," he said to me, "if I had been told that in a lecture on 'Le Barbier de Séville' there would be not a word of *Figaro*, I should never have believed it."

And he read me an indignant lecture.

"Monsieur," I replied to him, "a lecture must please the public and instruct it, that is evident; but it is also necessary that it should interest the lecturer. The one that you have heard is the third that I have given on 'Le Barbier de Séville;' in the first I did indeed speak of *Figaro*, of his ancestors, and successors; in the second I showed that 'Le Barbier de Séville' is the prototype of the vaudeville, as the writers of the Restoration understand it. This time, in order not to repeat or bore myself, I have taken *Rosina* and compared her to all Molière's young girls, and Regnard's, and those of the contemporaneous theatre. And that is why in a play of which *Figaro* is the very soul, the name of *Figaro* has scarcely been mentioned once."

The institution crumbled away day by day—it slowly fell in ruins.

Ballande finally retired. He obtained the concession of the Théâtre Déjazet, and there founded, with his habitual solemnity of language, the "Third Théâtre-Français." There I continued, together with Lapommeraye and some others, to give a few lectures, but they no longer drew a crowd; the taste for them had died out.

I had gained in this campaign, followed for several years, more or less knowledge of the trade, the ability to explain my processes to myself, and to acquire a more facile handling of them. Perhaps it will not be disagreeable to you if I take advantage of this pause to tell you what these processes were, to give you a little theory as to the lecture as I have understood and practised it.

VIII.

HOW TO LECTURE

I do not pretend to teach you how to set about giving a lecture. I simply wish to relate to you how I set about it myself; I wish to spare those who may read me some of the groping that I went through, to point out to them some of the rocks on which I have more than once foundered. I know very well that the experience of others is of very little use. Perhaps, however, these counsels, fruits of long practice, will have a certain interest for those who intend to follow the same career.

It is needless to say, is it not, that if you are to undertake lecturing the gift for it is necessary. Oh, I mean a little gift, a very little gift. It isn't a question of being born for great eloquence. A very fair success can be attained in this direction without an eminent collection of superior qualities; but, still, it is necessary to possess certain aptitudes, modest ones, if you will, but real. There are men who are very skilful writers, and even brilliant talkers, who will never speak in public. Some have not fluency, others have a weak, dull voice. Thirty years ago a great deal was said about the lectures of Alexandre Dumas, *père*. No one was more amusing and brilliant than Dumas chatting at table or in a salon; in a lecture and before an audience he was simply extinguished. He read, in a loud but indistinct voice, passages from his "Mémoires," and connected them with difficulty. The crowd came all the same, because it was greedy to behold the old Dumas in this new form. We journalists took care not to make any criticism that would chagrin this good giant, enamoured of popularity. He might believe, and he did believe, in all good faith that he was king of the lecture as he was of romance. There never was a more naïve soul or one more open to illusions. He never could have succeeded in this direction had he not brought to the lecture-table the radiance of his name. His voice was cottony; it made no impression on the audience.

But I need not lay great stress on this. On this point it is with lecturing as with all other arts. At the base there is the gift, that is to say, an *ensemble* of natural qualities without which one can never become, in spite of every effort and all the labor in the world, anything more than a good and neat workman: it is certainly something to be that, and as, after all, the lecture is not an art of luxury, as teaching is its end, and as it aims by preference at practical utility,

I should have scruples about discouraging worthy persons full of learning and good-will, who should seek by appropriating our methods to conquer natural obstacles.

The first condition in giving a lecture is to have something to say.

"To make a hare-ragout," says "La Cuisinière Bourgeoise," "first catch your hare;" a good hare-ragout cannot be made of a rabbit's tail.

But let us understand each other. To have something to say is not to possess upon the subject you have chosen new ideas or peculiar views; it is not to produce paradoxes, were they the most ingenious and possibly the truest in the world. No, I will say to you that, even if you have these new ideas, these peculiar perceptions, these paradoxical points of view—well, the advice I should give you would be to keep them prudently in your pocket, at least to be sure of the audience to which you address yourself, and to be still more sure of your authority over it. Get this primordial truth well into your head, you who aspire to the honor of instructing or amusing your contemporaries. With lectures people can only be taught that which they know, they can be persuaded only of the things of which they already desire to be convinced; only those ideas can be opened to them as to which they have been somewhat enlightened in advance; the good seed of the word germinates only when it falls upon minds long before prepared to receive it. Distrust every new idea that shocks an ancient prejudice, and above all a general sentiment; if you hazard it, do so only with extreme circumspection.

No, when I speak of having something to say, I mean that it is necessary to have upon the subject treated some ideas discovered for one's self, be these ideas as old as the world, be they simple commonplaces. A personal idea is not a new idea, there is not much original observation; it is an idea that one has discovered after many others by the effort of one's individual initiative. Originality consists not in thinking new things, but in thinking for yourself things that thousands of generations have thought before you.

Let us take an example:

You have to speak, we will suppose, of "Le Cid" by Corneille. Do not weary yourself at first by reading all that has been written on "Le Cid;" steep yourself in the play, think of it, turn it over and over, go to see it if it is being played; if neither the reading nor the representation of the drama suggests to you any impression that is properly yours—good gracious! my friend, what would you have me say? Don't meddle with lecturing either on "Le Cid" or any other theme drawn from literature. Manifestly you are not born for the trade.

But if you have shuddered and thrilled at a given passage, if there has been presented to your mind some comparison that has, so to speak, sprung from the depths of your reading; if you have yourself formed an opinion upon the whole, or upon some scenes of the work, you must cling to that, it is that which must be told, it is that that I call having something to say.

Do not trouble yourself to know if others have thought it before you, and have said it perhaps even better than you will say it yourself. That is not the question. The idea, however old it may be, will appear new, and will be so indeed, because you will strongly impress upon it the turn of your mind, because you will tinge it unconsciously with the colors of your imagination.

As you will have made it flash from the reading, as you will yourself have drawn this truth from its well, your passion will go out to it, you will naturally put into its expression a good faith, a sincerity, a transport, the heat of which will be communicated to the public.

Not until you have performed this first task, the only necessary one, the only efficacious one, shall I permit you—pay attention—permit you—not advise

How to Lecture

you—to read what your predecessors have thought of "Le Cid," and written about it. If by chance you run across some interesting point of view that had escaped you, and that strikes you, take care, for the love of heaven, not to transfer it just as it is to your lecture, where it would have the mischievous effect of second-hand and veneer. No, take up "Le Cid" anew, reread it with this idea, suggested by another, in mind, put it back into the text in order to draw it out yourself, rethink it, make it something of your own, forget the turn and the form given it by Sainte-Beuve, from whom it first came to your notice. If you cannot succeed in taking possession of it, in melting it so well in the crucible of your mind that it will be no longer distinguished from the matter in fusion which is already bubbling there, better discard it, however pleasing, however ingenious it may be.

Be assured there will be nothing good in your lecture but what you shall have thought for yourself, and what you shall have thought for yourself will have always a certain seal of originality. You have thought that *Chimène* sacrifices her love to her duty, that *Rodrigue* is a hero boiling over with love and youth, that *Don Diègue* is an epic Gascon. Do not embarrass yourself with scruples and repeat to yourself in a whisper, " But everyone has said that."

Everyone *has* said it! So much the better, because there is some chance that your audience will be enchanted, seeing you plunged up to your ears in the truth. But everyone has not said it as you will say it; for you will say it as you have thought it, and you have thought it yourself.

I cannot insist too much on this point. In the lecture the commonplace must not be discarded; I do not know who it is has said that the commonplace is the body and soul of eloquence. That is a great truth. But it is necessary to rethink the commonplace for one's self, to recast it, in some way, in the image of one's own mind.

Our professors—many have tried lecturing—have nearly all a defect against which I must warn them, for it is this defect which explains the coldness with which I have seen lectures full of erudition, of good sense and intelligence, received by the public. They never fail when they speak of a work to review the opinions expressed by the critics who have preceded them, discussing them, showing their strong and weak points, and concluding: "La Harpe said that, Villemain contradicted it, Sainte-Beuve ranged himself on the side of the first," and they quote, discuss, expand. It is an excellent method in a class of rhetoric or before a Sorbonne audience. In lecturing it is another thing. There is—there ought to be

How to Lecture

—nothing true but what the lecturer says; the rest does not exist. I, who listen to him, know neither Sainte-Beuve nor Villemain nor La Harpe; I see him only, and it is for him to tell me what I must believe. And the more what he tells me conforms to what I already believe to be true, the more will I discover of good sense and talent in him.

Regulate yourself accordingly, you who seat yourself in the lecturer's chair. You must clear away all that has been said before you on the subject that you treat.

If you assume, even intentionally, the ideas of others, you must have assimilated them—you must have made them your flesh and your blood. You launch them from the heights of Sinai, with the conviction of the prophet who has just seen the Lord face to face. It is the Lord himself who has revealed to you these marvellous truths: that *Chimène* sacrifices her love to her duty, that *Rodrigue* is a hero, and that "Le Cid" is a work which sparkles with youth. You are convinced of them, impregnated, on fire with them when you descend from the mountain. You are happy and proud to bring them to your audience. You impose them upon it.

I speak perfectly seriously, for I have a horror of irony, which is the driest and most sterile of figurative forms. If you do not draw from yourself (often after having put it there by design) the matter of your discourse, you may be able to make either ingenious salon chatter or severe Sorbonne lessons; but you will never—mark me well—you will never give a good lecture.

When once you are in possession of your subject, and of the ideas that it has suggested, they are then to be classified and arranged; that is the work of composition. I know none more important or more difficult. Doubtless when you were at college you learned by heart, or at least read the sermons of Massillon. You remember those geometrical divisions of implacable rigidity; this will be my first head, and that will be my second head, and that will be my third head. And the sermonizer took each of these heads, one after another, and when he had finished the first head, he did not fail to warn his auditors of it: "Notice, I pass to the second head." In the same way with the second head, and even with the third, which was nearly always the last.

You have smiled over the inflexibility of these limitations, if, indeed, you have not pronounced them a bore. Well, a lecture must be constructed and arranged like one of Massillon's sermons. It goes without saying that you can, and that it will be better to, conceal from sight the lines of this framework which distinctly mark its parts. But the lines

How to Lecture

must exist, you must have them always present to your mind and the public must feel you sustained by them.

A lecture has a chance of imposing itself upon the audience and pleasing them only when each hearer can say, if his wife asks about it: "This was his thesis, and to sustain it he said first this, then that, and finally that, in conclusion." I would almost lay it down as a law for this work that there is needed in a lecture only one leading idea, which is made clear and confirmed by three or four groups of successive developments.

Yes, but how to arrange these developments? I believe that there are some very clear and powerful minds that immediately find the most luminous and conclusive order; that establish, so to speak, at the first stroke, after a glance at the *ensemble*, the great divisions on which their developments rest. Happy they who have this force and directness of thought. I confess that in the preparation of a lecture, what I have always hit on last is the general order of the subject-matter and the arrangement of the developments.

As I imagine that there are among lecturers many as frail as I, who are not capable of embracing a subject at a glance, and dividing it into its principal parts before doing anything else, I shall tell how I went at it; I realize that the process is not the best one, and it has played me many a trick, but I give it to you for what it is worth, and it has continually been of great service to me.

I knew what I wanted to say, I had my ideas on the subject; feeling my impotence to arrange them I did not trouble myself with composition and I took one of the themes to develop by chance. I pondered on it, turning it over and over in my brain, without asking myself in what place it belonged. I did the same with the others, I took them as the caprice of my work brought me to them; I rolled them a long time in my head, and little by little, without my knowing just how, the large divisions disentangled themselves and became visible to me. The developments arranged themselves, so to speak, and took their true place—and I generally succeeded in establishing and determining the *ensemble* and the composition only long after having thoroughly prepared each of the parts.

There is one lecture that I worked over three or four times before different audiences before having discovered and fixed upon its best arrangement, the most logical and the clearest. It is true that when I finally possessed the true frame I considered the lecture done, the rest was for me only accessory.

It is a defect of my mind; I can only raise myself

to the *ensemble* by aid of the details. Buffon says, with reason, in his discourse upon style, that before beginning to write a work the plan must be very exactly determined. As for me, it is, on the contrary, in preparing the expression of my ideas that I succeed in discovering and fixing their arrangement. It is not the method of the masters, and my excuse is that I cannot do otherwise; and even now, after so many years of practice, when I have a lecture to give, I never trouble myself with the arrangement of ideas, reserving that to be reached later, as best may be; I throw myself immediately, heart and soul, into that part of the preparation which should come last, that which consists of seeking and fixing the form under which these ideas shall be presented to the public.

On this particular point of form and style, most dreaded by adepts in lecturing, I have some advice to give that may prove profitable to them. It is, first of all, never to read a written lecture, and never to recite a lecture learned by heart. You will tell me that some of the most celebrated men have done it, and you will recall to me what I have told you of Paul Féval, and Mr. Ernest Legouvé. You can cite more instances of it; Coquelin the elder reads his lectures, at least those that I have heard; and there are others, with fame not so far reaching. But notice: Paul Féval gave two lectures during his lifetime, Mr. Legouvé a dozen perhaps, Coquelin three or four; no one of them has pretended to make a profession of lecturing. I am supposing that you wish to become a veritable lecturer like myself, that is to say, a man capable of improvising, on no matter what subject before any audience, a development of any theme whatsoever. Very well, you could read or recite lectures for ten years, and you would not be trained to the profession of lecturing. You would not be any further along at the end of ten years than on the first day.

And then, if you but knew what force of persuasion is lost in reading or reciting. If one reads, the eyes, bent upon the paper, no longer open over the crowd to magnetize it; if one recites, the glance turns inward, hypnotized by the effort of memory, and no longer gives out that electricity which awakens and stirs the audience. Some seek to dissemble; they make a show of improvising that which they read from a corner of the eye upon a skilfully hidden manuscript; or they pretend to hesitate at a word of a phrase that they have learned beforehand and know by heart. These are tricks "stitched with white thread," which deceive but for a few moments. The audience are not long in seeing through the artifice; the development is too regular, the phrase is too complete and polished, the words themselves are too justly chosen or too ingenuous; all this smacks of and betrays preparation. It is better when one reads or recites to do it frankly.

"What need have you," asked I of M. Legouvé, "of that manuscript that you spread out on your table and the pages of which you never turn? You never look at it, and you possess an imperturbable memory."

"It is a matter of honesty and modesty," he replied; "I try to speak as if I were improvising, but I do not wish to give myself the airs of an orator who does improvise. I insist that the audience shall know the truth; it hears a lecture given by a man who knows how to read."

Coquelin still less makes any bones of it; he reads frankly, and in order that no one shall be ignorant of it, he puts on, that he may read more easily, the obligatory eye-glass.

It is not because he is lacking in memory! But he doubtless thought that there would be no illusion about it, even if he learned by heart and recited, natural and varied as his diction is; and he was right. Illusion is impossible.

But see to what one is exposed when one reads. Coquelin read one evening, at the Salle des Capucines, a lecture on the art of the comedian, and speaking of the great artists who had made the stage illustrious, he quoted the name of Régnier. You know that Régnier was his professor at the Conservatory, and that he encouraged his first steps at the Comédie-Française. At his name Coquelin stops, takes a moment of time, and says, in a broken voice: "Pardon, gentlemen, if I cannot overcome my emotion."

The action, if it had truly sprung from improvisation, would have touched the audience. But no! it was marked in advance: the orator said to himself "here I will be moved—my voice shall choke or break, I will be forced to suspend my reading for an instant."

It was, then, only the trick of the comedian, and instead of softening us toward the lecturer, we admired the art with which he rendered his part.

Never, then, write a lecture. I will even add, do not carry notes, at least in the lectures that I shall call state lectures, which are to be given before a numerous audience in a great hall. I would only admit notes in the lectures which, being addressed to a small audience of the initiated or faithful, resemble the college lesson. At the theatre or in the vast circular amphitheatres, no notes. Remember that the public is a monster of a thousand heads, and you can only control it by fixing your glance steadily upon its own. While you look for your paper and read it, the monster frees itself from the magnetism in which

How to Lecture

you have wrapped it. It has leisure to think of something else, and often takes advantage of it.

But the quotations?

Well, don't quote, or if you cannot avoid it, quote from memory. The quotation will be perhaps shortened, mutilated, stripped, so much the worse for the author. What is the author to you! He is dead, and you are on the stage. For you the essential thing is not to let go of the audience for an instant. I have spoken upon all the classical works in the repertory; you may well imagine that I do not know them all by heart! I have a most copious memory, it is true, but at the same time the most inexact in the world. I never bothered about it. When I had a quotation to make, verse or prose, I always resolutely launched the text at random, changing the words, falsifying the verse, as memory served; but what did it matter to me? Either the public knew the play, and the entire passage came to their minds in its true text, or they didn't know it, and in this case my quotation sufficed them perfectly, because it was absorbed and carried along by the development of the idea to which this quotation only supplied support and light.

I permit you only one note, but that I counsel you to bring and keep open on your table. It ought to be contained in a little scrap of paper as large as your hand.

This note is the plan of the lecture. There are three or four points which the lecture should touch successively, and which form, as it were, its skeleton; these points can be fixed by two words, let us say a line of writing, if you wish to give full measure.

You will very rarely have need of this scrap of paper, but it is a security to know that it is there. It happens to you often, doesn't it, in chatting with a person, to miss a name or a word that you need? The more you seek for it, the more it evades you, the more it recedes into the obscure depths of baffled recollection. And yet this name or word is familiar to you—you have it, as they say, on the end of your tongue. But it acts as though it did it on purpose—it will not come out.

Well, blanks of this kind often open up abruptly in the memory of a lecturer, one knows not why, in which the development disappears, swallowed up, body and boots.

When one has his idea, one is certain of being able to develop it, whether well or ill; but if the idea is lacking, one may search the memory in affright, it will no more yield you the absent idea than it gave you, in the previous instance, the lost word.

Do not rely upon reasoning to pick up the points

you have lost. First, it may be that the composition of your lecture is not logically excellent; it is, as I have warned you, the most difficult thing to find, and the thing found last if found at all, the fine order of the parts contributing each in its logical place to the harmony of the whole. If the ideas of which the lecture is composed are linked only by an artificial thread, it may be that this thread will break, and the ideas escape like the pearls of a broken necklace.

But even when the arrangement of the lecture is excellent, when the themes follow one another and connect logically to circulate around the principal idea, an unexpected bewilderment may be feared. There suddenly appears in the brain an enormous void—it is a frightful sensation of which I can speak with authority, for I have twice been a victim to it.

The first time I was obliged to leave the hall. It was so painful a spectacle that no one either laughed or hissed. The eye became suddenly vague and the glance wondering, the face was clouded. I drank down two or three glasses of water, one after another, stammered some incoherent words, and withdrew, staggering. The audience thought it a sudden attack of paralysis.

The other accident was much gayer. It was on the Boulevard des Capucines, before the restricted audience of the place, with whom I had long held familiar relations. I was amusing myself that time with improvising what used to be called "physiognomies," that is to say, professional monographs—the journalist, the dramatic author, the actor, the professor. It was a series that did not fail to amuse the habitués of the *Salle des Capucines*. I was speaking of the professor, and I had, according to the principles just explained, divided the lecture into three parts; to be a professor it was necessary to unite three things, which I had enumerated.

I develop the first theme, all goes well. Arrived at the second point the idea escapes me, it has fled, I cannot put my hand on it. But I am among friends. I do not give up, though such adventures are never without a suspicion of the ludicrous.

"Hold!" I say, gayly, "I can no longer find the second quality of the professor, it is a lost quality; is there anyone among you who can give it to me?"

They smile, there is no response. A word had been sufficient to set me going again. No one gives it to me; in fact, they appear amused at my embarrassment, which I conceal under a boyish gayety.

"Upon my word, gentlemen, I have certainly lost my second point. We will go on to the third. Perhaps the second will take advantage of the respite to return."

I enlarge complacently upon this third point, for

one can, when he knows his profession, lengthen and vary a development according to circumstance and time. But that imp of a second point is stubborn and will not reappear.

"Come, gentlemen," I say, with my customary cheerfulness, "I have not found the professor's second quality. Let us mourn it; I will go to-morrow to look for it at the office for lost articles. . . ."

And as everyone rose to leave, the idea came to me like a flash of light:

"Ah, gentlemen, I have it, I've got hold of it! . . ."

The movement is arrested; they look at me—they have an air of expectation; I draw out my watch.

"It has come too late; so much the worse for it. One should be on time."

They commenced to laugh, and that was all.

But since that accident, I always have in my pocket the four cabalistic words, with the aid of which I can recall the lost theme, evoke the vanished idea. It is a good precaution to take, and I advise you not to neglect it.

As for the developments, trust yourself only. I have told you never to write them. I am going to explain to you now how I went to work, how I still go to work to prepare them.

IX.

HOW A LECTURE IS PREPARED

When you have taken all your notes, when you have possessed yourselves of at least the substance of all the ideas of which the lecture is to be composed, whether you have them already arranged in fine order, or in the mass, still confused, seething in your mind; when you have reached the moment of preparation, when you no longer seek anything but the turn to give them, the clearest, the most vivid and picturesque manner in which to express them; when you are so far, mind, my friend, never commit the imprudence of seating yourself at your desk, your notes or your book under your eyes, a pen in your hand. If you live in the country, you doubtless have a bit of a garden at your disposal; and in default of an alley of trees belonging to you, a turn around the town where no one passes; if you are a Parisian, you have in the neighborhood either the Luxembourg or the Tuileries, or the Parc Monceau, or in any case some wide and solitary street where you can dream in the open air without too

How a Lecture is Prepared

much interruption; if you have nothing of all this, or if the weather be execrable, you have in your house a room larger than the others; get up and walk. A lecture is never prepared, except while walking. The movement of the body lashes the blood and aids the movement of the mind.

You have possessed your memory of the themes from the development of which the lecture must be formed; pick out one from the pile, the first at hand, or the one you have most at heart, which for the moment attracts you most, and act as if you were before the public; improvise upon it. Yes, force yourself to improvise. Do not trouble yourself about badly constructed phrases, nor inappropriate words—go your way. Push on to the end of the development, and the end once reached, recommence the same exercise, recommence it three times, four times, ten times, without tiring. You will have some trouble at first. The development will be short and meagre; little by little around the principal theme there will group themselves accessory ideas or convincing facts, or pat anecdotes that will extend and enrich it. Do not stop in this work until you notice that in thus taking up the same theme you fall into the same development, and that this development with its turns of language and order of phrases, fixes itself in your memory. For what is the purpose of the exercise that I recommend to you?

To prepare for you a wide and fertile field of terms and phrases upon the subject that you are to treat. You have the idea; you must seek the expression. You fear that words and forms of phrase will fail you. A considerable number must be accumulated in advance, it is a store of ammunition with which you provide yourself for the great day. If you commit the imprudence of charging your memory with a single development which must be definitive, you will fall into all the inconveniences that I have brought to your attention: the effect is that of reciting a lesson, and that is chilling; the memory may fail, you lose the thread, and are pulled up short; the phrase has no longer that air of negligence which improvisation alone gives and which charms the crowd. But you have prepared a half-dozen developments of the same idea without fixing them either in your memory or upon paper, you come before the audience; the mind that day, if good fortune wills that you be in train, is more alert, keener, the necessity of being ready at call communicates to it a lucidity and ardor of which you would not have believed yourself capable. It draws from that mass of words and phrases accumulated beforehand, or rather that mass itself is set in motion and runs toward it and

How a Lecture is Prepared

carries it along, it follows the flood, it has the appearance of improvising what it recites, and in fact it is improvising even while reciting.

This is not a new method that I am inventing. The ancients, alas! have worn the matter threadbare, and one must always go back to the *De Oratore* of the late Cicero. You have, I imagine, heard it told that Thiers, when he had an important speech to make in the Chamber, first tried the effect of his arguments upon his friends and guests. He received much company, and every evening he improvised, for a little circle of auditors, some parts of his future speech. Visitors succeeded one another, and he recommenced without weariness, and indeed without wearying them, the same developments. He was firing at a target. After all, isn't this the same kind of preparation that I recommend to you? You are not M. Thiers, you have not at hand a series of listeners, who relieve one another to give you a chance. I would not advise you to inflict the suffering of these recommencements and hesitations upon your unfortunate wife. Improvise for yourself, as if you were speaking before an audience.

It will doubtless happen more than once, in the course of these successive improvisations, that you will hit upon a picturesque word, a witty thrust, a happy phrase. Beware of storing it in your memory, and on your return, sticking it on paper like a butterfly fastened on a blank sheet with a pin. If you bring it to the lecture you will certainly wish to place it, and instead of abandoning yourself to improvisation in the development of your idea, you will be wholly occupied with directing it toward the ingenious or brilliant sally that you have stored away. You will appear embarrassed and awkward in spite of yourself, and three-quarters of the time you will spoil the effect upon which you counted. You will have sacrificed the thought to a *mot*, and the *mot* will miss fire.

That *mot*, heavens! perhaps it will not be lost, though you have taken pains to forget it. Who knows? Perhaps on some great day, in the flow of improvisation, it will mount to the surface, and you will see it suddenly spring up in the eddy of a phrase. Oh, then, throw it in boldly, it will be more attractive from having the air of a "find," a bit of good luck.

The great principle to which we must always return is that every lecture must be improvised; but have a care! one does not improvise successfully before the public until one has twenty times improvised in solitude, as one can only draw from a fountain the water that one has taken care to put into it beforehand.

How a Lecture is Prepared

Many believe that at least the exordium and the peroration may be learned by heart. It is not my opinion. I have tried it. I have never succeeded by that means. The most that I would admit is, in speaking before a new public, if one has first to address to it some of the phrases of courtesy and thanks demanded by custom, one may fix the expressions, because they are pure formulas of politeness; and it is better to know them by heart. It would be ridiculous to stumble in the phrase used to congratulate a person on his good health, or felicitate him upon his marriage.

But every time that you have true ideas to express—and they enter into the exordium and the peroration as well as into the rest—you must improvise. For the audience is always warned by a change of tone or manner of the moment when the author passes from recitation to pure improvisation, and it begins to be distrustful, it constantly wonders if the improvisation may not simply be an uncertain recitation; it loses confidence and resists. You see! there is no real success to be had—I cannot too often repeat it—unless the audience feels itself in some sort plunged, completely bathed, in the deep and rapid flow of improvisation.

Even the peroration—and between ourselves, is there any need in the lecture of what is called a peroration? The peroration is the bellow of the mediocre actor upon the last verse of the tirade. Great artists disdain the applause that it arouses. What do you undertake to do when you speak? You wish to explain and prove an idea. Well, when your demonstration is finished, you put a period to it—that is the peroration. The worth of a lecture is not in the ingenuity of an exordium, in the brilliant *fanfare* of a peroration, in the number and splendor of the lustrously cut phrases sown through the discourse; it is in the ensemble of its mass. Be sure that when you have faithfully explained, developed, and revealed your idea; when you have, with or without applause, impressed it upon the mind of your audience, there is no success comparable to that.

Applause! flee from it as from the plague. An audience that applauds is an audience that is not given leisure to listen. When it claps its hands, it's a sign that it no longer is bound to the idea that you express — that it is no longer carried away, rolled in the torrent of your discourse. It takes time to cry out at a pretty phrase, to go into ecstasy over a flash of wit—bad business for you! for it forgets while lingering to applaud this, that which is the foundation of the lecture, the succession of ideas and reasoning; you will have trouble in recapturing it again.

I am so persuaded of this truth that I never leave

my listeners leisure to breathe. Of course it has happened to me, as to my fellows, to touch here and there a corner of my discourse with a more brilliant vivacity than usual, and to be conscious of it; one is always conscious of that sort of thing. In such a case I hardly launched the last word of the development before setting out again at full speed for another series of ideas, cutting short all tendency to applause. The confidence felt in an orator evaporates in these bravos.

"*Le vrai feu d'artifice est d'être magnanime,*" said M. Belmontet once upon a time, in a verse still celebrated. The only applause that counts, the only true applause, is the attention of the audience, letting itself be so won by what you say that it no longer thinks of the way in which you have said it.

You will doubtless be somewhat alarmed to know that it is necessary to improvise a dozen times, and often more, each of the subjects for development of which a lecture is composed. You think to yourself that that is a tremendous task. Yes, my friends, there is nothing so long and so preoccupying as the preparation of a lecture; you must make up your mind to it, if you expect to follow that career. You will spend much time and pains on it. Reassure yourselves, however; the work will become easier and more rapid as the habit of doing it grows with you. Among these themes of development as each lecturer approaches only the subjects which relate to his studies and are within his range, some will often re-present themselves and will only require a summary preparation.

This *humus* of which I just now spoke to you, this prepared heap of turns of speech, of exact and picturesque words, will naturally grow richer; you will have it right at hand, and it will serve the occasion without fresh effort.

There will come a time when, even with themes that are new to you, you will no longer need, in order to establish the development, ten or twelve successive improvisations. You will be astonished to find with what facility, all at once, accessory ideas and convincing facts will spring from the first improvisation, and arrange themselves about the principal idea to sustain and clear it. It will always be delicate work, but it will no longer be so painful or so distressing. In a few hours, spread over two or three days, you will get through the preparation of a lecture, on condition, be it understood—it is a prime condition—of fully possessing your subject.

You have improvised—picking them out one after the other just as they came—each of the themes, so that it only remains to put them in their place on the day of the final improvisation. One of the great anxieties of a novice in lecturing is to know how to pass from one theme to another, what Boileau called the labor of transition—which used to give us blue terror in college. Permit me to give you, just here, an axiom which I only succeeded in formulating after much reflection and many attempts. In lecturing there is no transition.

When you have finished one development you enter upon another, as at dinner, when you have eaten the soup you pass to the entrée, and then to the roast. If there is no connection between the two ideas that succeed one another in your discourse, what use is there in an imitation of one? When you speak, distrust little strokes of finesse, tricks of style, bits of false elegance. All this is worth nothing and serves no purpose. When you have finished the explanation and the demonstration of the idea, say loyally, if you must say something, "We have done with that theme, let us pass to the next."

But the best way would be to say nothing at all, and to enter upon another order of development, with no warning but a short silence.

If, on the contrary, there is a connection between the two themes, do not disturb yourself, you do not need expressly to mark it. It is useless to take the trouble to throw a bridge between the two ideas; the moment that you, the orator, leap from one to the other, the audience must leap after you, borne on by the same impulse. The transition is no more than the movement of your thought, that the audience necessarily follows if you keep a firm hand upon it.

Ah! bless me, you, the lecturer, must have always present to your mind, even through any digression you permit yourself, your principal idea, and must not let your audience forget it; you will have no trouble in leading them back when you yourself return. And, if by chance you are so far removed from it that you do not know what road to take to reach it again, the simplest way is frankly to announce your embarrassment. "It seems to me that we are straying—where was I? Ah! I wished to demonstrate to you that—" and there is the thread picked up, without great art, I confess; but I have remarked that the public like very well to have you make a confidant of it, speak to it with open heart, if need be ask counsel from it. It would not do to make an artifice, a trick, of this means of exciting interest and sympathy. The public is very sharp, it would easily see that you played upon its credulity, and would range itself against you. But if you have truly lost the thread, do not fear to say frankly, "I do not know where I am—put me on the right track." If a word escapes you, ask someone to prompt you. They probably will not do so, but you

How a Lecture is Prepared

will have had time to find it while they search for it, or an excuse for not having found it any sooner than the others. This excuse would not be permitted to a man who recites, for it would pass for a failure in memory, and to be brought up by a defeat of memory is the worst that can happen in lecturing, as in the theatre and in the pulpit. Laughter breaks forth invincibly. It never offends in an orator who improvises, it may even please by I know not what air of sincerity and good fellowship.

Is there a special tone and style for the lecture, as there is for academic discussions, for the pulpit, for the Sorbonne, for the bar? That is a point to be looked into.

What is a lecture? It is, properly, to hold a conversation with many hundreds of persons, who listen without interrupting. It may be said, in general, that the tone of the lecture should be that of a chat. But there it is—there are as many tones for chatting as there are people who chat. Each one talks according to his temperament, his cast of mind, his turn of thought; each talks as he is, and that which is pleasing in a chat is precisely the discovery in it of the physiognomy of the talker. I can give you only one piece of advice on this point: try to be through art, when once seated in the lecturer's chair, that which you naturally are in your drawing-room, when you talk with five or six persons and when you engross the conversation. Hear yourself speak, observe yourself—these introspections are become very easy to us, thanks to the habit that we have contracted of analyzing ourselves—and bend all your efforts to producing a lecture, not according to your neighbor, who, perhaps speaks better than you, but yourself, only yourself, accentuating if possible the rendering of your principal traits. I will condense my counsels in this formula, which is not so humorous as it seems: It is permitted you, it is even recommended to you, to have a "make up" for the lecture, but the "make up" must be your own.

Your entire personality must shine forth in your discourse. And that is the especial service rendered by this method of successive improvisations that I have just prescribed for you. While you are thus improvising alone, face to face with yourself, without any witness to inspire you with a desire to pose, you are free, you unconsciously set your entire being in full swing. The mould is taken, you spread your personality before the public, you are no longer a more or less eloquent, more or less affected orator—you are a man; you are yourself.

To be one's self; that is the essential thing.

Among the young lecturers discovered in these later times there is not one who has more quickly acquired a greater or more legitimate reputation than M. Brunetière. Nevertheless there is not one further removed in speaking from the ordinary tone of familiar conversation. It would seem that the lecture, as he practises it, would hardly come within the definition we have given of the species—a conversation with an audience that holds its tongue. But what would you have? That is the way that Brunetière talks, and he talks as he is. He is a man of doctrine, who loves to dogmatize; he feels an invincible need of demonstrating that which he advances, and to force conviction on those who hear him. He manœuvres his battalions of arguments with a precision of logic and an ardor of temperament that are marvellous. The phrases fall from his authoritative lips with an amplitude, correctness, and force to which everything bends. He is to be found entire in his lecture—the lecture is, then, excellent, because it is of him, or rather, because it *is* he.

Old Boileau had already expressed these truths in some verses that are not among his best known:

"*Chacun pris dans son air est agréable en soi ;
Ce n'est que l'air d'autrui qui peut déplaire en moi.*"

If I should try to talk like Brunetière, I should be execrable; it is possible, on the other hand, that if Brunetière tried to appropriate some of my methods he would not succeed, because, to tell the truth, my air of good-fellowship, my familiarities of language, my jovial anecdotes interspersed with frank laughter, my unpolished and torrent-like phrases are not methods, they are all of a piece with myself; it is all I—a little more I perhaps than I ordinarily am, but Brunetière is also probably a little more himself in his lecture than in his chimney-corner at home.

May I be permitted to end these reflections on the art of the lecturer with some practical advice?

Never dine before the lecture hour. A soup, some biscuits dipped in Bordeaux, nothing more. If you fear gnawing at the stomach, add a slice of roast beef, but without bread. Do not fill the stomach. There is a rage in the provinces for inviting you to a gala dinner when you have a lecture to give. It's the worst of all preludes. It is in vain to try to restrain yourself. You eat and you drink too much; you arrive at the lecture-hall chatting with the dinner company. You have infinite trouble in recovering yourself.

Dine lightly and alone an hour beforehand, stretch yourself for half an hour on a sofa and take a good nap. Then go, entirely alone, to where you are expected, improvising, reimprovising, pondering upon your exordium, so that when the curtain rises you are in perfect working order, you are in form.

How a Lecture is Prepared

I do not know how the political orators manage to deliver their long discourses after gala banquets. It is true that they generally do not dine. I have seen those who all during the repast abstractedly roll balls of bread under their fingers, and only respond vaguely with insignificant monosyllables to the tiresome talk of their neighbors.

Speak standing; one commands a fuller and stronger voice, but especially the audience is dominated; you hold it with your eye. Speak from behind a table, even though (according to the rules that I have laid down) you have no notes to read, no quotation to make, book in hand. One is sustained by the table, and brought around to the conversational tone. If one has before him the wide space of the platform, in proportion as one warms up he makes more motions, he surprises himself striding across the stage; the voice rises and is soon no longer in harmony with the level of the things that are to be delivered. Beware of these balks. Watch the play of your physiognomy and your gestures, but not too much. I leave mine to the grace of God; what is natural, even though it be exuberant and trivial, is worth more than a factitious and studied correctness.

Have I other recommendations to make? No, I truly believe that I am at the end of my list. All the rest can be put into one sentence: "Be yourself."

It is understood, is it not, that it is necessary first to be some one? You now know the processes which I have used, which I still use. It only remains for me to end this history by telling you of the lecture in the provinces and abroad, and finally, in one chapter, which will be the last, of the campaign that we made in the Boulevard des Capucines.

X.

IN THE PROVINCES

If I consulted only the interests of my vanity I should refrain from writing this chapter of my memoirs. The excursions that I made in the provinces have left me but wretched recollections. I have never brought away with me very positive success, and it is only rarely and by exception that I have returned satisfied with myself and others. But the history of these failures, which have been numerous and constant, may be useful to those who follow the same career; it will spare them perhaps some of the shipwrecks in which I have been submerged, by pointing out to them some of the reefs on which I have been shattered. After having long spent upon the provinces a useless and very foolish ill-humor, I realized the causes which had kept me from succeeding, and I am convinced that in this affair it is I who have always wronged the public.

And first, my friends, cram into your heads this truth, which I have attained but slowly and after much reflection: Every time that a lecturer does not get firm hold upon the audience before which he speaks, it is his fault and not that of the audience; he can—he ought to—lay the blame only upon himself. You treat the audience when it has remained cold as idiots and blockheads. Be it so; I concede to you that your audience was what you say, but it was your place to know it and to manage yourself so as to say to them what would be understood by them or please them. You complain of their stupidity, but you are more stupid than they, since it was your business to foresee, to have a sense of this stupidity, and to accommodate your discourse to it. In the lecture as in the theatre (more than in the theatre, for the man of the theatre has the right to appeal from Philip drunk to Philip fasting; the lecturer has not that resource. If chance has it that he speaks before Philip drunk, he must take account of this drunkenness, and he must find just the things that will persuade and touch a king under the influence of wine), in the lecture it is always—and the rule admits of no exception—it is always the audience that is in the right as against the orator, for the final aim of the orator is to play upon his audience and lead it to believe or to do that which he wishes. If he misses his stroke it is because he did not aim accurately.

When your professors teach you rhetoric, do they still speak to you of rules of oratory? I doubt it, for I no longer see Cicero's "De Oratore" among the class-books. All the chapters that the ancients have written on the rules of oratory, and they have not been stingy with them, can be summed up in the formula that I have just given you. When one has to do with an audience of blockheads, it is necessary to know that one is going to speak to blockheads, and to say to them only what is calculated to win over blockheads.

You recollect the celebrated *mot* of one of the great lawyers of our Parisian bar. One of his friends who had just heard one of his speeches reproached him with having insisted upon an argument which was an evident absurdity. "When one is pleading," he answered him, "it is necessary to give bad reasons with good, there is always among the jurors a stupid mind that is touched by them alone."

This is really what the ancients—who have said everything there is to say about eloquence, their favorite art—called the rules of oratory ; to know by a sort of intuition the character and disposition of the audience one addresses and to take it at its sensitive points.

It is this fact, simple as truth and old as eloquence, that I have finally discovered after Cicero and Aristotle. But mark—one never discovers anything that Cicero or Aristotle has not said. Only it is one thing to have learned it from them, another thing to have found it out after numerous personal experiences, by means of study and reflection. And the proof is, that if, after having read this page, it happens to you to make a dead failure in lecturing, you will cry in an aside regarding the audience: "Blockhead!" while I, like you, will say: "Go blockhead!" but will mean myself. That is the difference, and it shows plainly that I am as well up in the rules of oratory as Cicero.

It was under the Empire, about 1865 or 1866, that I commenced to be in demand in the provinces. I do not know if lecturing has flourished there since that epoch, and it is of small consequence. I do not pretend to be writing the history of the lecture in our country. I lack the documents. I am recounting my recollections as my memory presents them, and trying to draw from them some lessons useful to my brother-lecturers. I did not trouble myself overmuch at this first period, which reaches to 1870, with the failures that I encountered nearly everywhere. I had foreseen and counted on them. I was not the less sensitive to them, but I said to myself that I could only get possession of the public of the provinces after many attempts and much groping. Workmen have a proverb which says that one learns the carpenter's trade only by spoiling much wood; one

In the Provinces

only learns the lecturer's trade by failing in many lectures. I spoke at that time at Nantes, where I was for two days, in succession, frankly execrable; at Lyons, where they were polite, but frigid, to me, and the truth is I was very mediocre; in some cities of Normandy and the East, and each time I felt, under the obligatory compliments of those who had called me there, the chagrined astonishment of people deceived in their expectations. But I had made up my mind. I had allowed myself some years to achieve the victory over this new public. I suffered no failure to dishearten me, however grievous it was to my *amour-propre*. I consoled myself by telling myself that the reverberations of it were limited and the echo would never reach Paris. The journalists of the locality, in courtesy to a colleague, accompanied the reports of the lecture with some hackneyed praises, that, of course, amounted to nothing.

After the war there was a great demand for lectures in the provinces. The municipalities organized some; in many of the cities there were formed literary societies, whose aim was the establishment of intellectual centres of instruction and conversation. The University was aroused; associations composed of professors of *lycées* arranged successive courses, some designed for young girls, others for people of society, others again more especially reserved for working-people. The idea naturally came to nearly all these societies to join to the lectures regularly given by the amateur orators the relish of a lecture by one of those who passed at Paris as masters of their art.

I was quite conspicuous just then; the lecturer's campaign that I had ostentatiously led in the Ballande matinées had brought my name forward. To me, then, most of the cities wishing to organize a series of lectures naturally addressed themselves. I was asked to deliver the opening lecture, or at least a special lecture. I believed the hour of revenge had come. I was master, or nearly master, of the trade; I enjoyed an incontestable authority; I had in this department that which M. Bourbeau lacked—prestige; I possessed a considerable stock of lectures already prepared upon the old repertory, and upon dramatic theories from which I could draw. It would be the dickens to pay indeed, said I to myself, if with all the trumps in my hand I did not win the game.

I continued to lose, time and again, as in the earlier days. They were not scandalous failures; no, just decent falls, the secret of which I should have been able, if I had had less clear-sightedness and more vanity, to conceal from myself. I felt, indeed, that everyone, upon returning, said at the club or café: "Was that all? It wasn't worth making such a rumpus about. If we had known, we should not have bothered to go."

Besides, I had one infallible criterion for measuring the extent of the disaster. When I had once spoken in a city they never asked me to return. I was burnt out for that place. Among all the cities into which I have carried the lecture, hardly more than two or three have asked me to return, and even then without appearing to be very anxious for it.

In vain I piqued myself upon my philosophy. You may imagine how long I kicked against that fatality which brought so many failures tumbling about my head, and how I laid my defects at other peoples' doors, instead of seeking the cause within myself. What would you? One can't be perfect, and the *amour-propre* is always there — watching, counselling you to blame the public and attribute to it the stupidities of which you alone are culpable.

It would be idle to relate to you the details of these mishaps. I prefer to unfold to you the causes, which I only discovered long afterward.

There were some particular ones which occurred only because I found myself in a special situation, and spoke in circumstances which could scarcely ever be the same again. You remember that at that epoch the religious question had taken on a keen interest. Gambetta had, in his powerful voice, sent forth his famous cry: "Clericalism, that is the enemy." I was writing under the leadership of Edmond About for the *XIXᵉ Siècle*, and we both launched almost daily against the clerical party articles that were very lively, very gay, very amusing, which all the Republican journals of the provinces vied with each other in reproducing, and of which the vogue was prodigious. It was a pleasantry which had passed into a by-word that I breakfasted in the morning on a curé and supped in the evening on a monk. The truth is that I never had such a disordered appetite. As to that I fall back on About's *mot*, who said, laughing, that if I hunted the unclean creatures I did not eat them.

I continually told those who came to engage me for a gala evening, that I never under any pretext touched upon religion or politics in lecturing; that I limited myself strictly to the domain of pure literature. They would not believe me; they winked smilingly at me. The ladies, who set the fashion, agreed together that they should not come, or if they came it was in a hostile mood. I had always a little clique of nice young people who kept their eyes open for the least mistake, the least occasion to protest or to laugh. And what grieved me more was that Republicans came to the lecture with the secret hope that I would find a way to give the enemy—Clericalism—its deserts; they also waited for a phrase, an allusion, to applaud. I had, indeed, a dim idea of the disposition of my audience, but even had I had a clearer perception of it I should not have been the less embarrassed, for I had, on principle, decided to refrain.

I remember, apropos of this, a little occurrence which enlightened me upon this state of mind that I vaguely suspected without being able to realize it clearly. I had gone into a town of Normandy to give a lecture on the "Polyeucte" of Corneille. The audience had been more than cold, and I had reaped on returning to the *foyer* only the flat compliments and lax pressures of the hand that mark for the orator and actor who are testing the temperature a sorry number of degrees below freezing. It nevertheless appeared to me that I had been good enough and in working trim that day. Some days after, on receipt of the local journals, I found the explanation of that frightful lowering of the temperature.

The Republican journalist rated me sharply for not having shown that "Polyeucte," in overturning the statues of the gods, had given way to one of those impulses so customary with clerical fanaticism. Ah, what an admirable opportunity I had had to stigmatize intolerance. Everyone in the town had believed that I had chosen that subject to strike at these eternal promoters of disorder. But I had failed. Doubtless I had been frightened by the young clergymen who had invaded a part of the orchestra. But I had nothing to fear; they were prepared to sustain me; I could have—I ought to have—gone ahead.

I swear that on reading this article I was stupefied, like one of Corneille's simple heroes. The idea, which appeared to me the height of buffoonery, had never once entered my head, to take "Polyeucte" for a clerical Turk's head to strike at in a lecture! But what completed my stupefaction was that in opening the Catholic journal I read that I had purposely lowered, by the familiarity of my language, the grandeur of a divine subject; that they perfectly understood this bad faith, the more venomous that it bore the air of *bonhomie*, the eternal enemy of all holiness and all religion, etc., and it proceeded to drag me through the mire.

I was struck at from both sides. For that, heaven knows, I cared not a fillip. I had had blows rained upon my shoulders until my skin was hardened. It defied that of the hippopotamus, to whom I sometimes had the honor to be compared in the sheets that prided themselves on their wit. But what astonished me most was that no one had come to the lecture to seek what they had asked me to give;

In the Provinces

what alone they had the right to expect, a lesson in literature. There had been misunderstanding, and, in consequence, disappointment. That, however, was not my fault. I had been faithful to my engagements; it was the audience who unconsciously failed in theirs.

Such circumstances, happily, are rare enough. The best way is, when one sees that one is about to be involved in some such situation, where one can neither overcome nor evade the difficulty, the best way is to keep out of it. It is what I ought to have done, and what I have done in some towns where I was told that religious feeling ran very high. In vain might I have cried upon the roof-tops that I did not regard anti-clericalism as an article of provincial exportation. I was impregnated with an anti-clerical perfume so violent that it exhaled even from my silence.

But if I have owed some failures to these special circumstances, others can be imputed to myself only, who have never known how to take the measure of the public with which I had to do in the provinces, and to whom I am prevented by pride and sulkiness from yielding.

Deputations, generally considerable, came from a town to seek to engage me upon the reputation of my name, for a lecture. I ought to have been able to say to myself from merely this first indication:

"Attention! these worthy people expect to treat themselves to a gala evening. I must not go to them in frock-coat with an every-day mind. To answer their expectations I must dress up my speech a bit; they are coming to hear a virtuoso; he ought to give them his *Carnival of Venice.*"

You can see from all that I have said to you of my manner of lecturing that the best qualities of which I have given evidence are *bonhomie* and familiarity; but every quality has its defects; I easily pushed the one to triviality, the other to too great freedom. I lacked balance. In Paris no one cared. When the Parisian public has adopted an artist, it accepts him *en bloc*, and permits everything to him. They said of me: "That is his way. We must take him as he is." They chaffed me sometimes for my freaks of language; but as I made up for them by an extraordinary sincerity and fervor of speech, they were not offended by them. These defects were part of my being, they had accepted them, some very indulgent persons even found them pleasant.

I knew these defects very well, for feeling it impossible for me to correct them entirely, since they belonged to the nature of my mind, I studied to compose a personal manner for myself. If I had had two cents worth of good sense and reflection I might have known that this would not work in the provinces as in Paris. These new audiences knew nothing of me but my name; I had not had the leisure to form relations with them, to accustom them to the excessive familiarity of this manner. I had not as yet enough authority to impose it upon them at the very start. When it did not wound their sense of propriety, it shocked them by a negligence that they took for contempt. How many times I have seen on the following day in the papers giving an account of the lecture: "M. Sarcey has not seen fit to take much trouble for us. He has not thought it worth while, doubtless, having to do with provincials," etc. And I received my switching.

And it angered me. I had, on the contrary, taken a great deal of trouble, for there is nothing so difficult—it is the height of art—as to chat with twelve hundred people as if from one's own hearth-stone. But I was a fool not to be willing to understand the state of mind of the public, who were eager to hear me, and not to manage to please them. I could have accomplished it somehow; I have done more difficult things than that. But I was in a temper. I, too, committed the unpardonable blunder of being angry with the public when I was the sole culprit. The most amusing, and at the same time the most mournful thing about it was that I blamed Lapommeraye, who was very much liked in the provinces, and who scored only triumphs there. Heavens! how little philosophy philosophers have. I passed fifteen years raging against others before recognizing the very simple fact that I was only an imbecile.

I hardly ever go any longer into the provinces; age and the multiplicity of my occupations keep me at Paris. I truly believe that now, if I went to give a lecture in some town, the authority that I have gained by thirty-five years of labor is such that they would accept me as I am, without retouching. But I have become wiser, and I accommodate myself to the requirements of the good people who do me the honor to listen to me. I cut out of my manner all that would not please them. I have made over for my use the chapter of Cicero on the rules of oratory.

I suffered still another inconvenience in the provinces. You know that I was for a long time a professor, and that I am still attached at heart to the University, whose doctrines and interest I have always defended in journalism. I was sure, then, when I came into a town, to have in the audience all the masters of the Faculty or of the School, who came less to learn—they knew as much as I—than to give a

In the Provinces

pledge of sympathy to one of their own. To this little kernel of literary hearers were added most often all those who in the provinces have a taste for things of the mind—magistrates, lawyers, high functionaries. It was a difficult audience, but open and receptive. Unfortunately they formed only a small portion of my hearers. Of what elements was the rest of the hall composed? Of curious persons come to see the face of a man whose name was in the papers, of women desiring to show themselves in theatre toilette, of worthy people animated by the best intentions but knowing not the first word of the subject to be treated, of victims of *ennui* who had no other aim than to kill a moment's time. A very composite audience of great disparity. Imagine a race-horse harnessed in the same shafts with an old cab hack.

Naturally I thought first of the little clan of my colleagues and their like; it was to them that I spoke. I indulged a certain coquetry in bringing to them a new view, or at least a personal view, of the drama which they had themselves profoundly studied. I avoided the commonplace as I should the plague, knowing that it would disgust them. What foolishness! I ought to have thought that they were intelligent enough to understand that if I were addressing myself to a large audience it was to the large audience that I should speak, and that I was bound in honor to tell these only what they would understand, while they, ill prepared to accept new truths, would not accept them and would even be annoyed at having them presented.

It is folly for an orator to despise the commonplace, especially when he has under him a heterogeneous audience.

I gave but one lecture at Marseilles. It was at the Grand-Théâtre, in 1871 or 1872, a short time after the war. A large lottery had been organized for the benefit of the widows and children of the victims: I had been asked to speak, and I had taken for a subject our sorrows and sufferings during the siege of Paris. I had recounted with much simplicity and emotion the phases through which we had passed, and it seemed to me that I was listened to with attention; the audience had appeared to be amused when I had spoken of some of the comic incidents of the siege, they had been touched in the sadder portions, when I had recalled our distress.

The evening ended, however, in the coldest fashion, and the crowd retired with an air of disappointment which I could not mistake: I knew it so well.

I had down there a college friend, Parisian by birth, education, habits, and who, at Marseilles, where he occupied an important position, remained Parisian to the tips of his fingers. We had been great friends at Massini's, and we kept up a correspondence after he left the *lycée*, so that to him I opened my heart.

"It's a complete failure, isn't it?" I asked him.

"No," he replied. "Not precisely. But do you know what your lecturing lacks, and what causes that impression of coldness that you have remarked at the end? It is that you finished as you commenced, and as you continued, in a simple and uniform tone. They listened to you with much interest, they were even amused, but you failed to rouse them at the last moment by a brilliant tirade. They expect an explosion of blind partisanship, of fine-plumed phrases, of resounding words, a bunch of fireworks; nothing more would have been needed to fire the hall—a Marseilles hall."

"I thought of it, in truth," I said to him. "But I knew there were half a dozen of you Parisians there, and I did not dare."

"Ah," he responded, "it is precisely because I am a Parisian that I understand how necessary it is to speak to the Marseillais in the Marseilles tongue."

He was right. I had long had a horror of seeming to make phrases. Experience led me to juster views on this point. The rapid and sounding phrase is certainly in itself a bad thing, and one to be guarded against. But it is a sign of a too exclusive taste, it is poorly to understand the necessities of eloquence to banish it altogether from the discourse.

I had been one day to give a lecture at Coulommiers, at the invitation of Marquis de V——, who had also been one of my companions at the Lycée Charlemagne. I had spoken in the afternoon, and he begged me to remain all night; for he had at dinner one of the most celebrated lecturers of this age, and Bancel, after dessert, was to occupy the same chair that I had occupied some hours before. I had never heard him; I accepted, although urgent business recalled me to Paris. I cannot here criticise either the manner or the talent of Bancel, who is now dead. If the volume in which he has published a collection of his lectures falls into your hands, you will easily see that the idea is nearly always absent; there are sonorous and magnificent phrases which he launched with an inspired air, in a resounding voice, striding across the platform, with forcible gestures.

I confess that he did not please me. On the morrow, after his departure, I chatted with my host as we walked up and down the paths of his park, and I told him the scorn that I felt for these rhetoricians who sought effect only in the magnificence and sonority of words.

"Well," said he, "you are wrong. There is

In the Provinces

Bancel, who had yesterday for hearers some *petits bourgeois* of Coulommiers, and a large number of peasants whom I had caused to come. It is clear that they did not comprehend much of his discourse, which passed over their heads."

"Oh, I believe you!" I cried.

"But believe me, these words, these grand words of liberty, progress, civilization, flung at them with a strong voice, awakened their minds, incited them to think, to reflect, opened to them a world of ideas which had, up to that time, been closed to them. These words, doubtless, have the same meaning for them as for us, even though perhaps not a very clear one; they don't know exactly what it is; what matter, if it moves them, warms them, and, as Rabelais says: '*leur désemberlucoque l'entendement?*' To raise them from the purely material interests in which they are sunk, to furnish them with a subject of conversation and discussion, is that nothing in your opinion?"

"I wish," he added, "that you had the time to go about with me just now in the neighborhood. I know all these worthy people; you would converse with them, and you would see if I am right. You have said very good and very just things to them, and things that they have understood. You have not shaken them like Bancel, who has told them nothing at all, but who has said it with conviction and energy, in fine, sonorous phrases. Words, you see, words must not be disdained when one is an orator, for words govern the world."

To govern the world! It is a great business! I have been content to instruct it, and, when I could, to please it. I have told you how and why I never pleased it in the provinces. I had more luck abroad.

XI.

IN FOREIGN LANDS

Belgium, Holland, and Switzerland are the European countries which offer the largest hospitality to the French lecture. All good society there speaks our language easily, and even in Belgium, at least in all the Walloon portion, French, which is the official language of the country, is freely employed in the ordinary relations of life. I do not believe that in England one of our people has ever been able to organize a course of lectures. I have heard of lectures given by M. Renan or M. H. Taine, or by M. Pasteur, but they were formal occasions arranged for a famous man by the academies or the universities. I have in all my life given but one lecture in London, and that was entirely by chance. I have an amusing recollection of it, because among all that I have given, in France and abroad, it is the only one that brought me money.

I had come to London with the company and, so to speak, among the luggage of the Comédie-Française. M. Mayer, the impresario with whom the

Comédie-Française had arranged, offered to put his theatre at my disposal between four and six for a lecture. He would bear all the expenses, and the expenses once paid, we would divide the receipts. I had nothing to risk; I was not much entertained by London, where the days were sometimes long; I accepted.

I arrived at the hour set. No one, or almost no one, in the hall. Mayer informs me with a contrite air that we have unwittingly chosen a day of the races; others tell me that the lecture had been insufficiently advertised, that the places were too dear; the true reason is that in London I was not known by the public at all, and the public had not considered it worth while to put itself out and pay half a pound to hear me. It is the only reason that was not alleged. There was all the same a little something made out of it, because two or three boxes had been taken by some considerable personages who wished to give a mark of sympathy to a Frenchman, but who did not push their courtesy to the point of occupying them. In France we take concert tickets in the same way for a Polish pianist, and then remain in our chimney-corner, while he taps with all his might upon a hired Pleyel.

When I had finished my "brilliant piece" and left the stage, I saw coming toward me a gentleman whom I had remarked in the first row in the hall, for he appeared to listen with much attention. "Monsieur," said he to me, "I am manager of the *Nineteenth Century*, the name of which you perhaps know." I did in fact know this review, which was then, and doubtless is now, one of the most celebrated in England. "Your *conférence* has interested me keenly. Are you willing to give me the manuscript? I will have it translated, and I am convinced that all our subscribers will regret, after reading it, having lost the opportunity of hearing you."

I was a little provoked by the indifference of the English public; it was an unexpected revenge that was offered me. I was only too glad to grasp the opportunity; but the manuscript that he asked for— I had it not! and I told him that I never wrote a word of my lectures.

He appeared surprised. "That is not the custom with us," he said; "our lecturers, as the name implies, always read or recite. But this lecture," he added, obligingly, "you ought to know it; couldn't you write it?"

I weighed my response, for it was a big task, and one which did not seem to me very convenient to be undertaken in a hotel room. He misunderstood the cause of my hesitation.

"It is true," he said, "that the expense of translation being ours, we shall only be able to pay forty guineas for the article."

"Forty guineas!" That figure staggered me. A guinea is worth a little more than twenty-six francs. It was something like eleven hundred francs that he offered me for a piece of work that would have paid me two hundred francs in France.

"When will you need the copy?" I asked.

"Day after to-morrow."

"You shall have it without fail."

"All right!"

I had taken for my subject the organization of the Comédie-Française, it was a sufficiently curious piece of work, full of personal views, and was much to the taste of the English public. The best proof of the success that it obtained is that the manager of the *Nineteenth Century* asked me for a study upon the Theatre of the Palais Royal as a pendant to this article, under just the same conditions, of course. It pleased less, not because it was less careful, or less piquant; it seems to me, on the contrary, that it had more flavor. But the translator, who was a great friend of mine, had been arrested by a difficulty that we had neither one of us suspected. The French language has, for the purpose of expressing the ideas of the pertly witty badinage upon which the repertory of the Palais Royal has subsisted for years, a crowd of words and turns of speech, of which each has its particular shade of meaning, from the simple bit of gayety to the most unbridled buffoonery. All these words, which are like the colors of the palette, I had used according to the kind of piece of which I was speaking. You can imagine my stupefaction at seeing appear at every turn in the translation the word "licentious," which awakens in the mind the most disagreeable images of gross immorality.

"What would you have?" Barbier asked me; "the English do not know this kind of pleasantry; they have a horror of it. They have no words in their tongue for the shade so varied, so fine, so delicate which '*grivoiserie*' admits of with us. *Grivoiserie, grivois* have no equivalents with them, any more than *égrillard, gaillardise,* and many others. They put all into the same bag, or, if you prefer, into a single word, which testifies to a morose and indignant virtue, rather than to a mind agreeably tickled, and in humor to laugh."

We confided our scruples to the manager of the Review, who did not share our apprehensions. Some days after I quitted London and heard nothing of it. But Barbier told me that this study was a closed book for the English.

My lecture at the Gayety Theatre, that lost lecture, did not bring me less, indirectly, than two thousand six hundred francs. I could not have made so much at home in ten years of lecturing. You will do me the justice to realize that in these souvenirs I have never approached the question of money. Permit me, since the opportunity presents itself, to say a word about it. I shall not be suspected of speaking *pro domo meâ*, for I am very nearly out of the field, and like the old Entellas of Virgil, *cœstus artemque repono*. I am not defending my own interest. I no longer have any in this affair.

It is a sort of tradition in the provinces to offer a lecturer no suitable compensation. Many a society in a large town does not hesitate to allow a singer or a dramatic artist, who comes to recite a bit of verse, a payment of five hundred or even a thousand francs. I see no harm in that, assuredly. But some day it prefers to treat itself to the luxury of a lecture. It offers the man it chooses just the wherewithal to pay his travelling expenses; it is, so it tells him, simply for that purpose.

Nevertheless, the lecturer is nearly always a considerable person in his way, very much occupied, and who is sought for the sole reason that he has won a wide reputation. He is asked to quit his business, to lose a day or two of his time, which is precious, to do a very risky and fatiguing piece of work; I do not know any labor more exhausting than that of lecturing, which demands the highest exercise of strength, and the greatest expense of nervous fluid ; and people think to be even with him—what am I saying?—it is believed to be a sort of favor to offer him a sum which is merely a reimbursement of his expenses.

In Paris, we were not paid, or so little that it is not worth speaking of. But in Paris we were at home ; there was no inconvenience or loss of time. And then, Paris is Paris. The notoriety reaped from the lecture was payment in itself; "play" money, if you will; but that kind sufficed at Paris, where it was current. It was another affair in the provinces ; no money and no favor! What then?

How often, at the epoch when lecturing in the provinces was at the height of its great vogue, some of my younger confrères came to me and said : "The lecturer's recompense is absurd. Your age and your authority would permit you, and you only, to impose other conditions. You will render us all a real service by taking the initiative. The price once raised by you, we shall profit naturally by the increase."

I had at various intervals chatted on this question with Lapommeraye, who more than I, in lecturing at least, held the ear of the provinces. Lapommeraye was of the opinion that we could make this attempt together. But I had never considered lecturing as anything but an amusement; I hardly saw in it a calling. Often an impresario had come to me and said: "Would you be willing, with such a subject as is indicated to me, and which is the order of the day, to make a round of lectures in the departments? There is not a shadow of expense, the municipality will almost everywhere put a hall at your disposition, the newspapers will gladly give you publicity, you need trouble yourself about nothing; we will divide the receipts." The proposition never failed to be tempting. I always refused. It has always been repugnant to me, I do not know just why, thus to coin money with speech. It is a prejudice, for there is no reason for not profiting by lecturing as by a *feuilleton*, one is as legitimate as the other. I found it more dignified to be invited either by the municipal council, or by a literary society, of which I became the guest. Only I could wish that they have less respect for us, and that they treat us, I do not say on the same footing as the actors—my ambition does not reach so far as that—but as good workmen, to whom one pays what they are worth, whenever they are engaged.

In Paris, some of the impresarios, who in these later times have organized lectures, have resigned themselves to offering an appropriate remuneration. I believe that certain towns are commencing to follow

In Foreign Lands

their good example. The lecturers who come after us will be more fortunate than we have been. We have planted the vine, they will gather the grapes. But possibly, in eating them they will taste less pleasure than we have done in making them grow. We have created, or at least have acclimated, an art. When, glancing backward, I consider the enormous amount of time and strength devoted to lecturing that has brought me next to nothing, others in my place might complain; but I—no. I have taken more pleasure than the cost in money. I have still been the gainer.

Belgium and Holland are the only countries in which I have exercised the industry of lecturing. I should have liked to make a tour in Switzerland, where some of my colleagues told me they found a very serious, very attentive, and very sympathetic public. But I should have to go at my own risk and peril; rent the halls, take care of the advertising, install a ticket-agent, and these housekeeping details are too wearisome to me. In return, I had been asked, with many repetitions, to come to Copenhagen, where a fine reception awaited me; I had nearly accepted, when at the last moment my heart failed me. In the same way I could have gone to St. Petersburg. I had given my consent. But it was under the auspices of one of the grand-dukes that the first lecture was to be given, for which I had graciously promised to come. A funeral in the family postponed the project, which was never taken up again.

I was at the same time somewhat sorry and glad. The idea of venturing a lecture before an audience of princes and *grands seigneurs* sent cold chills down my spine; I could not picture myself, a peasant of the Seine, holding forth in the midst of that illustrious assembly, so I experienced an inexpressible relief when I learned that I should be spared that trial; and, nevertheless—man is truly an abyss of contradictions—I was heart-broken at not being able to fight that battle.

Would you believe it? An American impresario proposed to me, as though I were Coquelin or Sarah, to take me to South America and have me give a round of lectures there for him for three months. I looked him in the eyes to see if he were making fun of me. But no, he was as serious as a pope; so serious, even, that he offered to deposit at the bank half of the sum that he promised me. I dare not tell the figure; you would think I was fooling you. I believed myself that he was fooling me. It was ten months to pass far from Paris, in the most outlandish country, to seek problematical success; and to catch yellow fever. I shirked it!

Belgium is less doubtful, and it is at hand. It was

not at Brussels that I first made acquaintance with the Belgian public. It was in one of those little colliery villages, to-day desolated by strikes, but which were then tranquil and prosperous : at Marchiennes, not far from Charleroi. There was, it appears, the same rivalry between Marchiennes and Charleroi that we sometimes see in France between two neighboring cities, Beaune and Dijon, for example, Sens and Auxerre, Marseilles and Aix, which seek to do each other bad turns, and riddle each other with epigrams. Marchiennes, to outstrip Charleroi, had instituted a literary and artistic society that gave concerts and lectures, and prided itself on inviting thither celebrated virtuosos.

The president came to see me. It was at the time when I was carrying on the anti-clerical campaign with the greatest ardor in the *XIXe Siècle*. The Marchiennes *cercle* was entirely composed of liberals, and you know the question excited even more lively passions in Belgium than in our country. From among the subjects that I proposed to him, he chose, you can guess why, the pamphlets of Paul-Louis Courier. Edmond About had just opened in the paper a subscription to raise a little commemorative monument to the wine-grower of la Chavonnière ; I had my Paul-Louis at my fingers' ends, so all was for the best.

This president was a very amiable man, very hospitable, as everyone is in Belgium, and he received me with open arms. Scarcely landed, I found the table loaded with food, and all about joyous companions of marvellous spirits, who seemed to have agreed among themselves to make a festival for me. They urged me to be seated. You know my principles, I never dine before a lecture. But I let myself be won over by their vivacity and gayety. It is in Belgium that our best growth of Burgundy is drunk. I excused myself in vain, I must fill my glass and touch it all around. They ate to drink, and they drank like bellringers, and I assure you the conversation took a pace! They execrated Messieurs the Clergy, they told stories of them to make you die with laughter, or to raise the hair on your head with horror.

"Hit hard," said the president, "and set at it in earnest. I answer to you for a proud success."

The heady gayety of these good people, and perhaps also a finger of Burgundy — Burgundy is a treacherous wine — had intoxicated me a little. Nevertheless, it was not my intention to "hit hard," as my host advised. It did not seem to me suitable for a Frenchman to come into Belgium to sow discord and mix himself up in polemics that did not concern him. I promised myself, then, to be very moderate, and I was. But what would you? I had to do with an audience that saw allusions in every word, caught them on the fly. When I pronounced the name of the Jesuits, however little malice I put into the intonation, the audience were shaken with a mighty laugh. It was the public who gave the lecture, for which I was only the pretext, and it found it excellent, admirable. It clapped its hands; it would gladly have borne me home in triumph.

"Now," said the president, "we must have some refreshments."

He takes me to a room of the club, where I find some forty persons seated silently at table before some bottles, waiting for me before drinking. We mount, the president and I, upon a platform of honor, and I say in a low tone, not without some alarm: "Ah, am I to be obliged to give another lecture?"

I was soon relieved of anxiety. All my dinner companions were there, they started talking again, and there was an exchange of outrageous pleasantries —a chapter of Rabelais's "Gargantua."

"But drink," the most animated said to me. "What a poor drinker you make!"

And in truth they swallowed down pint upon pint. The parched sand of the desert does not sooner absorb a shower of rain. I declared that beer was not my favorite drink.

"Ah, my fine fellow! You like Burgundy better. Let us have some Burgundy!"

I trembled, but had to submit. The company was broken up and we went to our host's house. The table awaited us, fully set, and loaded with old bottles. There were hams, pâtés, and cold fowls, as at the wedding of Gamache. It was midnight when we sat down to sup. I wished to eat only a chicken wing; there was nothing for it; their opulent gayety went with their opulent repast, and set me going a little in spite of myself. Those venerable bottles, each with its date, were no sooner opened than they were drained. I was astonished, with an admiration mingled with alarm, at the amount of Burgundy the Belgian stomach is capable of holding. I ended by begging for mercy.

"You doubtless prefer Champagne?" my host said to me.

I looked at him with fright; we had been drinking Burgundy for two hours.

"Let us pass on to the Champagne," he resumed, with a shade of regret.

It was in vain for me to protest, they declared it to be impossible to end a supper without drinking a "*flute*" of Champagne. A "*flute*," my friends! Trombones rather, *ophicléides* of Champagne were poured *à la ronde*. Four o'clock struck.

"'Pon honor! gentlemen," I said. "I can do no more, I must go to bed."

"It won't do to quit like that, in three or four hours it will be day!" I stuck to it. My mind was firmer than my legs. I mounted to my room, pursued by the friendly shouts of those intrepid drinkers, who—I being gone—set themselves to work again as before.

On the morrow I awoke at eight o'clock. I must take the ten o'clock train to Paris.

I dressed and descended to the dining-room. I gave a cry of surprise. They were still there. The table was strewn with empty bottles, there remained only the crust of the pâtés; the bones of the fowls, scraps of galantine, the scattered débris of a Pantagruelic feast.

"Ah, there you are!" cried the leader of the joyous band. "We can breakfast together."

I made so forcible a gesture of negation that they all shouted with laughter.

"Nothing sets one up like a glass of old Burgundy."

And I must sit at table again, whether or no, with these *bons vivants* and cope with them. Ah, the worthy people, wearing their hearts upon their sleeves, a gayety of such "*haute gresse*" and such warm Burgundy! How they animate an audience for you, what a whirlwind of enthusiasm they bring into it! I went into the country again two years afterward. My host unhappily had been taken ill and died. He was a very distinguished physician; he knew, I was told, that he was condemned to an early death, and he had wished to put to the profit of friendship and pleasure the little time he had to live. He was the soul of that association, which after him went to pieces.

You may imagine that I did not find in other centres of Belgian population the same habits and the same expansive Rabelaisian gayety as in this little privileged corner of the earth. But everywhere I encountered the same kindly humor, the same taste for large hospitality—often more than large, luxurious—the same desire to be agreeable without the vulgarity of tame compliments. In my relations with the Belgians, and I visited in lecturing the greater number of their large cities, I have always met with fine and smiling cordiality, the audiences appeared very responsive, and upon the bad days very courteous.

For I have had my bad days in Belgium as everywhere. Of my successes I shall not speak — why should I?

Yes, I won great successes down there; my first lecture at Brussels was one of my finest triumphs, and I never remember it without pleasure, for truly upon that evening I was satisfied with myself; and I believe that the audience, which was numerous, was pleased also. But of all the cities in which I have oftenest succeeded, the recollection of Liége gives me the most pleasure. What a charming population! so literary, so amiable, so truly French, with a something—I know not what—more serious and better balanced to their minds than we always have! It is my regret, when I think of that amiable public, that I am no longer nimble enough in body or lively enough in mind to go among them and refresh myself with a little familiar chat; for this familiarity, which is the mark of my manner, did not displease them, and I felt myself as free with them as with a Parisian audience.

What a bother it is to grow old! But, as some one says, it is as yet the best way that has been found for living a long time.

XII.

IN HOLLAND

It was the year that France organized a universal exposition at Amsterdam. When I say "France" it is a form of speech. It was a French company that took the lead in the enterprise. Some distinguished members of the Parisian press were invited to be present at the inaugural festivities. M. Dietz-Monin had begged me to join the party. I had never seen Holland, I accepted with pleasure. You know that we journalists can do nothing without announcing it by trumpet blasts, *urbi et orbi*. My name appeared in all the papers together with the names of my companions, the hour of our departure, and the reception that awaited us.

Some days before leaving Paris I received a letter post-marked Amsterdam. A Hollander who called himself my confrère wrote to tell me that he had seen in the newspapers that I was to take part in the expedition; he offered me the hospitality of his house, excusing himself for the great liberty; he proposed to be my guide and cicerone for the curiosities of the city. The letter was signed Van Hall.

That letter was very prettily turned, full of *bonhomie* and kindliness. But when one is a Parisian, and still more a journalist, one has seen so many things of so many kinds that one learns to mistrust. Perhaps this was simple practical joking, perhaps again this hospitable Hollander was one of those terrible bores who, the grappling iron once thrown upon the victim, no more release their prey than does the greedy Acheron. At the idea of putting myself into unknown hands from which I could not withdraw, I trembled from head to foot. I responded to the signer that I regretted my inability to accept his invitation, but that we were to depart in company and were pledged not to separate from one another.

The journey was very gay, and we installed ourselves, everyone of us, in the same hotel where we had engaged rooms. The day after my arrival the hall-boy brought me the card of a gentleman who asked to see me. I took it and read "Van Hall."

"Botheration! my bore!"

I gave orders to introduce him.

I beheld a man of amiable countenance, easy manners, who spoke French with an extraordinary purity, not a shadow of accent, in whom I immediately felt confidence. He proposed to me to take a turn through the city; we chatted familiarly, and I was surprised, and at the same time enchanted, to discover in this Hollander a Parisian of an alert mind, very familiar with our literature, knowing the boulevard to the tips of his fingers, and, as we say, "*dans le train.*" He invited me to dinner for that evening. I went to his home. I found a charming family, who welcomed me with the most cordial simplicity. It seemed to me at the end of an hour that I was with friends of twenty years' standing.

After dinner I ascended to my host's study. I admired the library, in which our contemporary poets occupied a large place.

Mr. Van Hall was a great admirer of Coppée, several of whose poems he had translated into Dutch. Quite half of this library belonged to German literature, for the Dutch, besides their native tongue, all speak—at least in the better classes—German and French with the same facility. I was somewhat ashamed of our ignorance, seeing this man who chatted with me of Meilhac's last play, instruct me upon the literary movement in Germany, upon the theatre of Berlin or of Vienna. I was confounded by this agile curiosity, this taste for exact information, this open-mindedness, this smiling grace.

"Well," said my host, when I took leave of him

to return to my hotel, "are you reassured now? Oh, I understood very well that your excuse was only a pretence. You were afraid, confess?"

"Well, put yourself in my place."

He opened a door.

"Here is your room," he said to me. "It awaits you; to-morrow I will have your trunk brought, and you will be at home here."

I passed with this excellent gentleman a delicious week, of which I shall retain the most vivid and charming recollection all my life. In the long talks that we had together the question of the lecture and lecturers naturally came up.

Mr. Van Hall told me that some years before Coppée had made a lecturing tour in Holland, and that his success there had been immense; there was a regular rush for him; he had repeated some of his best poems, and all the women were captivated both by the verses and by him who read them.

"Do you want to try next year?" he asked me. "I have charge for the Art Club of the literary entertainment evenings. I will arrange for you the same course as Coppée had: Amsterdam, Leyden, The Hague, Utrecht; you shall see how you will be received everywhere!" I made some objections; indeed, I had been so bruised by my recent mishaps in Belgium that I was still used up; and I trembled at the idea of confronting a new public, a public that scarcely knew me at all; while in Belgium I was, thanks to the anti-clerical campaign in the *XIXe Siècle*, almost popular when I decided to speak there. Mr. Van Hall did his best to reassure me, and the truth is, I only asked to be convinced. The idea of returning, of pressing once more those friendly hands, of finding myself again among these peaceful and hospitable surroundings, attracted me. I promised. It was agreed that I should return to Amsterdam toward the first of May. Later I should have had no hearers, as society in Amsterdam went out of town; earlier, I should have had to submit to the severity of the cold weather, which is bitter in Holland. Mr. Van Hall told me entertainingly of the imprecations of poor Coppée, who is very sensitive to cold, against the climate of the country. The unfortunate man shivered under the enormous fur-lined cloak in which he was enveloped from head to foot. He looked desperately at the snow; his face disappeared under the silk scarfs that he knotted, one above the other, about his neck. There is, he once told me, no heat in that country except in the hearts of the people.

As I had been told that the Dutch are naturally very serious-minded, I had thought it would be best, in order to please them, to choose my subjects from the classic dramas, and to entertain them rather with the austere masterpieces of Corneille and Racine. I took then "Polyeucte," "Horace," "Athalie," "Le Misanthrope," "Les Femmes savantes," and, if occasion offered, "Le Barbier de Séville" or "Le Mariage de Figaro," writing Mr. Van Hall, who was to be my guide in this affair, and begging him to point out himself the plays that appeared to him the best fitted to appeal to a Dutch audience. I have learned since that he would have preferred subjects that were less grand and belonged more to the present; but he said nothing of it to me, fearing to trouble me, and assured me that I would be listened to with pleasure, whatever the theme of the lecture might be. So I chose "Polyeucte" and "Le Mariage de Figaro."

I had adopted, for speaking of the master-pieces of classic drama, a method which is current to-day, but which at that time was entirely new, and perhaps savored slightly of scandal.

This method rested upon a very just idea: Corneille and Racine, studying to paint the human heart, had put upon the stage the universal, and even the eternal, passions of humanity. *Oreste, Phèdre, Agrippine, Polyeucte, Horace,* doubtless had different customs from ours, and expressed themselves in a language that we no longer speak; but they felt as we do; they loved, hated, suffered, wept, and laughed precisely as we do to-day.

In order, then, thoroughly to comprehend and enjoy classic works, it was necessary to seek the passions which move our own souls under the poetic phraseology of the seventeenth century. It was necessary, if I dare use the comparison, to transpose the antique work as one plays a scrap of music in another key; it must be brought into the current of contemporaneous life.

I was not, you may well believe, the first who had had this idea. In criticism nothing is invented. But a theoretical idea that one does not draw out of the domain of speculation to give it practical application, hardly touches the imagination. It is as though it did not exist. To say in a general way, for example, that *Agrippine* is a mother jealous of the authority she exercises over her son, and that there have always been, as there will always be, jealous mothers, fond of authority, is to say nothing great, and does not teach anything to anyone.

The curious, the difficult part is to take the action and the characters of a classic work, boldly to transport them into modern surroundings, and to show in the *Pauline* of "Polyeucte," or in the *Hermione* of "Andromaque," the woman with whom you dined the evening before, and to whom you sent a bouquet on the following day. It is to render the discourse that Corneille and Racine lend to their heroes, in familiar and contemporaneous prose, letting drop occasionally some verses of the original text, so that the resemblance and the contrast shall break suddenly upon the vision of all.

It is one method, I grant, but it would seem to be a method not very easy to handle, for, since I have given the formula and example of it, I have seen some of my confrères try it timidly, and fail pitiably. It needs a touch of a surety, an adroitness, and even a delicacy, to which it is very difficult to attain.

The speaker who executes this transposition must all the time allow the original work to show through it, and manage in such a way that this very familiar, almost trivial, translation of an heroic text shall appear so true, so profoundly true, as not to shock the prejudices of a literary audience; he must, moreover, execute it with such quickness and good humor that the audience shall not have time to collect itself and resist. I need hardly say that some of these analogies between the antique work and the modern life will be forced; that is an inconvenience of the system, it cannot be avoided. So the audience must be subjugated, taken into the plot, borne along, as it were, on the whirling utterance.

All the tragedies of ancient times do not lend

themselves to these translations; thus there would be no way of modernizing "Le Cid," or, if one should do it, it would be only a puerile piece of wit. But I have thus transposed, and often with prodigious success, "Horace," "Cinna," "Polyeucte," "Mithridate," "Athalie," "Britannicus," and still others. I have written some of the lectures, and I have made Monday *feuilletons* of them for *Le Temps*. Theatrical amateurs may possibly recall the three *feuilletons* in which I amused myself by drawing *Athalie* out from the surroundings in which Racine had placed her, and throwing her into the midst of the nineteenth century. They amused my readers much, and I had the pleasure of finding later, in all the classical editions that have appeared of "Athalie," some of these ingenious and suggestive comparisons quoted with commentaries by the grave professors of the University.

I need not tell you that no one in Amsterdam suspected this system of analysis, nor the effects of surprise and laughter that could be drawn from it. And that was fortunate for me. I have several times, in the course of this narrative, told you how my ignorance of the secret sentiments of my public had injured me. It was only just that this same ignorance should once have turned in my favor and rendered me service.

Upon seeing the posters, all the Dutchmen (these details were given me afterward) said to themselves that they were going to be bored in the correct fashion, listening to the panegyric of an austere classical work. The name of "Polyeucte" could never have awakened sportive images in their minds; they resigned themselves to the hour of attention that social propriety imposed upon them. Many of my audience had re-read Corneille's tragedy the preceding evening, and yawned to themselves. But it would have been unbecoming to confess that they had not fully enjoyed a work consecrated by the admiration of centuries, and reputed to be a masterpiece.

I mounted the platform; and in a few moments I had despatched the theoretical portion of the discourse, which appeared to pique the curiosity of my hearers. It chanced that evening that I was in capital spirits, master of myself and quite at ease. I reached the essential part of my lecture, which was also the dangerous part. I took *Pauline,* and supposed her to be one of the young Dutch girls who were then before me, and then——

I need not repeat that lecture to you here, since I gave it again two or three years ago, at the Odéon, before a full house which appeared to enjoy it greatly. I only wish to tell you about the impressions of that audience. There was first some hesitation and some astonishment; the dissimilarity between what they had expected from a study of "Polyeucte," and what I was giving them, was so strong, that the audience, disconcerted and wavering, did not know whether to be frankly amused, or whether it would be more proper to be angry; for, after all, with my audacity of disrespectful familiarity, I resembled that iconoclast of "Polyeucte," who broke the venerated idols, and that could not be suffered.

Happily I had among my hearers, without counting Mr. Van Hall himself, some professors of the University, and among them a man who, by his wide knowledge and good taste, enjoyed an incontestable authority in the city. He was reputed to be grave, very grave, having given up his entire life to works of erudition, and he was so indeed. But he had wit, and he saw immediately, through the intentional exaggerations of these analogies and contrasts, how just was the fundamental idea, and that it required rare analytical and oratorical art thus to follow it scene by scene, and render it visible to the eye. He gave the signal for applause, and was pleased to smile at some happy hits; the entire audience began to clap their hands with him and to laugh with all their heart. The women, enchanted at not being bored, dared acknowledge themselves amused, and once set loose and fairly launched, they did not stop. "Polyeucte" had never had such a reception in Holland, nor doubtless anywhere else.

On the morrow the public got possession of themselves, and some objections came to light. Was it not treason to Corneille to inflict this translation, which was only a travesty, upon him?

"Heavens!" I said to people who spoke to me thus, not without sincere trouble. "You may believe that I know what there is excessive and even false in these transportations. But mark, if I had pronounced, in a more or less brilliant fashion, the panegyric that was expected of me, everyone would have applauded and praised me, and no one on the morrow would have given thought to Polyeucte any more than though it had never existed. You acknowledge yourselves that you have passed your day in re-reading the work of the old master, that the women themselves are moved, that it has been for twenty-four hours a subject of conversation and even of dispute in the town. I am right, then; for I have for an hour given animation and action to a tragedy congealed during two centuries in an unmoved admiration."

There was much to answer to these arguments; but you know nothing succeeds like success. I had everyone for me, even those who grumbled through respect for the tradition lightly overturned. I was very happy to have succeeded so well, first for myself, for thus I won a name in Holland; and then for my host, Mr. Van Hall, who had answered for me, and who was not without some uneasiness as to the issue of the enterprise. For when a lecturer brought from such a distance fails, it is always the organizer who gets the blame. The lecturer goes away, but the organizer remains, and it is he who suffers from reproaches and ill-humored jokes.

I went in this campaign, borne on by the fame of this first success, from triumph to triumph. I had the pleasure of speaking, in one of the towns of Holland, before an audience composed solely of students. The students down there form a vast association which is extremely rich. It has had built for its own a sort of hotel or palace, where its members meet to read, to drink, to play. There are libraries, billiard-rooms, a café, and finally, what most concerned me, a hall for lectures or plays which was magnificent and comfortably fitted up. Nothing could be more cordial and kindly than the way in which these young people received us, Mr. Van Hall and myself. I feel some shame in recalling the delicate attentions with which I was loaded, the eulogies and compliments that I received. What charmed me more was that in me (they made it plain) they honored France and the French language. That is, indeed,

In Holland

the joy and the peril of these expeditions upon foreign soil. One may thoroughly realize himself to be nothing great, but he feels all the same that, in whatever degree it may be, he represents the country, and if he commits a blunder, it is she who suffers for it, as she is raised in the estimation of the people he is among if he is fortunate enough to please them.

I returned to Paris worn out and good for nothing. I had spent a week speaking nearly every evening, which would not be very fatiguing, but also in taking part in the gala suppers that followed the lectures, always on exhibition, talking and toasting. I had some trouble in recovering from this excess of fatigue, and when, the following year, Mr. Van Hall urged me cordially to return to Amsterdam, telling me that everyone there was asking for me again, I responded that I should be happy to see his fireside again, to seat myself once more on that veranda from which one beheld in the distance such fresh rolling verdure, but that I intended not to quit Amsterdam: I would give two lectures there, three at the most, each followed by a day of rest.

It was thus that things were arranged.

Nevertheless, I had my little failure there that year, for I was fated to have one everywhere. Oh, a very little one, this time, which did not assume disastrous proportions. If I relate it, it will be as a new proof of that truthfulness upon which I have already insisted so often in this long autobiographical study on the art of lecturing. It is necessary before addressing an audience to inquire very exactly into what it expects, what it desires, what it fears, to feel out its tastes—in one word, to observe the "rules of oratory."

You recall that lecture that I gave in London for the organization and history of the Comédie-Française. I imagined, I don't know why, that the subject would take in Holland. I was in thorough possession of it, I may say I was full of it. I did not trouble myself to prepare developments, sure that when the day came they would come in crowds to my mind. Upon this point I was not mistaken. The lecture was full and solid, and even here and there enlivened by ingenious hits. It had no effect; the audience remained depressed.

I perceived it, not without astonishment; for it did not seem to me this time that I was below my average. But I soon had an explanation of the mystery. The Dutch, when they read from the posters that I was going to speak to them of the Comédie-Française, all said to themselves: "A man who has amused us so much with such a severe subject as 'Polyeucte,' will overcome us with laughter when he opens to us the mysteries of the theatre he has known so intimately and practically for so many years." They had come with the idea that I was going to give them portraits of artists, relate anecdotes to them, put them *au courant* with the theatrical cuisine. They expected to be put in good spirits and diverted. I ought to have suspected it; it was so natural in them.

But no; I brought them a dissertation, interesting certainly, but very severe in tone and aspect, upon the organization of the Comédie, upon the decree of Moscow, and the hindrances it had received; there was nothing very gay in all that, and, it must be said, nothing that had any great interest for the inhabitants of Amsterdam, who know of the Comédie-Française only its fame, and care not how it is governed. I should doubtless have had a lively enough success with this lecture in Paris, at the Salle des Capucines, or with Bodinier at the Cercle d'Application; I should at least have been listened to with interest and sympathy; I bored the Dutch, and it was my own fault.

It is true that, once advised of my error and its causes, I took two signal revenges. I gave in particular, before an exclusively masculine audience—the audience of a club which had invited me expressly to speak—a lecture upon the passion for play in the theatre, which is among the best that I remember, and I have reason to believe that it is not yet forgotten in Amsterdam.

The rumor of the always kindly, sometimes enthusiastic, welcome that I received in Holland, was spread at Paris through our little circle of lecturers. Many of those who prided themselves on belonging to it, came to me to get information as to the pecuniary arrangements made with orators, and, as they were very fine, for Holland is larger and more generous than Belgium, they prayed me to intercede with Mr. Van Hall. I did so. None succeeded. But I had warned them discreetly, so far as it was permitted me, being one of their set and open to the suspicion of throwing obstacles in their way through jealousy; I warned them that the Amsterdam audience, like that of The Hague, of Leyden, and of Utrecht, was doubtless very courteous, but very cultivated, very intelligent, difficult, delicate even, demanding absolutely the solid and the good, whom it is not permitted to treat lightly.

But what would you have? These young people have a curious inclination to believe that foreigners are only too happy to see a Parisian, to crowd about him, to listen to him, and to welcome open-mouthed every word that falls from his lips. There were some mistakes made. These mistakes had, unhappily, the effect of cooling the desire of the Dutch for lectures.

In Holland

Mr. Van Hall wrote me that things had reached the point where only my name or that of some brilliant personality, such as Émile Zola, or Alphonse Daudet, for example, was capable of drawing a numerous audience to a lecture hall. There had been too many and too cruel disappointments. The Dutch had vowed never again to go to hear a Parisian lecturer, at least not unless he was of the highest rank.

I let a year go by myself without going back; the list of journals for which I wrote was ever lengthening. It became nearly impossible for me to leave Paris for a week in winter; and I no longer felt the same elasticity of mind and body as formerly. I have never again beheld Amsterdam, or Brussels, or Liége, of which I keep such pleasant memories. I believe that courses of lectures in the provinces and abroad are now ended for me, unless upon some extraordinary occasion, under exceptional circumstances: "*Vétéran, je m'asseois sur mon tambour crevé.*" And I remain in Paris, where I shall gather faithful audiences about me sufficiently often, in the Boulevard des Capucines.

I will end these memoirs and this study by the account of my twenty years of assiduous lecturing in that hall. Reassure yourselves, it will not be very long now.

XIII.

AT THE SALLE DES CAPUCINES

I shall not here undertake to recount the full history of the Salle des Capucines. I am poorly acquainted with it; lectures were always given in the evening there; I have never been able to follow them closely, since I am by profession on duty at the theatre during those hours. For the rest, my purpose in writing these purely personal memoirs has only been to tell what I know of this profession, and to open to young beginners, by showing them my successes and my mortifications, the treasure of my old experience.

It was after the war that the little society of literary people and of lawyers of which I spoke at the beginning of this work, carried the lectures of the Rue de la Paix into this hall of the Boulevard des Capucines. This hall was not too well chosen: its only advantage was its situation in the very heart of Paris, in the richest and most populous quarter of the city. But it was dull in aspect: it had to be sought out at the rear of a court; it

At the Salle Des Capucines

could only be reached through a narrow door and a dingy hallway. It was small, with low ceiling, cut with great pillars, robbing a portion of the audience of the view of the platform. All the audience were on a level floor, seated on chairs which stretched away like rows of onions. The spectators could not see one another, and it was impossible to establish among them that electric communication without which an audience is never anything but a collection of isolated individuals, who feel a languid pleasure in listening to an orator, when, indeed, they are not heartily bored, each by himself. In addition, the hall was badly lighted, and badly heated; one's feet were frozen by a current of cold air, while the head, congested, was bathed in an atmosphere much too warm. This wretched hall has been my despair for twenty years. The interior arrangement has been somewhat improved during these last years, without rendering it, alas! more convenient or more cheerful. I am convinced that the *ennui* that is breathed there and the discomfort that is inflicted upon the audience, have largely accounted for the slight attention manifested. Lecturing has not succeeded, for want of a spacious and comfortable home. I have never been abroad, where I have found such beautiful amphitheatres, without returning melancholy to our poor little black, sad hall of the Boulevard des Capucines.

The directors who succeeded each other there felt its faults, surely, but they lacked money. They could not think of building a proper hall, because they got no receipts; and they had no receipts, because they had no hall. It is a vicious circle from which they have not escaped, and within which we are struggling still at the hour of my writing. If only we had on the Boulevard des Capucines the hall which Bodinier has constructed on the Rue Saint-Lazare, where he gives sometimes theatrical representations, sometimes lectures, and occasionally even lectures that are only a kind of theatrical representation! But we should need two hundred thousand francs at the lowest figure; and two hundred thousand francs will never be found at a lecturer's disposal.

At the time the lectures of the Boulevard des Capucines were opened, I took quite an active part in them without binding myself to regularity—which was moreover not asked of me. There were, without counting myself, Messrs. Chavie, Deschanel, Flammarion, Lapommeraye, Frank Géraldy, and others besides, whose names I no longer recall, not having listened to them, who came in turn to set forth their ideas; and as the institution then had the grace and piquancy of novelty, the audiences were numerous and faithful. Some of the orators, better liked, more conspicuous, filled the hall, Deschanel and

Flammarion in the first rank. I gave, at this time, a series of lectures which appeared to please the habitués; I remember particularly having amused them by improvising for them a series of monographs of professions: the professor, the journalist, the dramatic author, the lawyer, the magistrate, and others. But all that could not go far. When one has not a fund of consecutive teaching to sustain lectures, subjects cannot but fail; fancy soon exhausts itself. The lecturers in fashion grew more and more scarce. Deschanel, appointed to the Collège de France, reserved himself naturally for his chair and for the state. It was difficult to find speakers, and speakers commenced to find their audience more sparse and restive. This precarious situation rightly gave the director concern.

He came to me, one morning, to unfold a project which he had long meditated. He proposed to arrange with a few carefully selected lecturers, who should pledge themselves, each, for once every week or fortnight; it would be, so to speak, a regular troupe, which would assure him a certain number of evenings, gathering an audience of faithful habitués for an expected lesson upon fixed days. The *bashibazouks* of the passing days would fill in the voids.

He had thought of me to give each week a lecture upon the play that should have been given in one or another of the theatres—a sort of spoken *feuilleton*. He developed his idea, which appeared to me very specious, with much warmth. But I had my reasons for not going into it.

"Listen," I said to him; "I have no desire to give a lecture upon the drama each week. I have already my Monday review for the *Temps;* every time I am asked for an article or for a lecture, a subject that bears upon dramatic art is proposed to me; I receive at home only the people who talk about the theatre; I go to the theatre every evening; I am up to my ears in the theatre."

As I spoke I saw his face lighten; an enigmatical smile hovered about his lips, and, instead of insisting, of urging me, as I expected, he asked me to whom I thought he could address himself for this work.

"I scarcely see anyone," I told him, "except Lapommeraye who could do you this service. He is as well acquainted with the theatre as I am; he speaks fluently and easily; he is liked by our public."

My man broke into laughter.

"What are you laughing at?" I asked; "what is so amusing?"

"If I laugh," he responded, "it is because I have just come from Lapommeraye. I may indeed tell you now that I thought first of him, foreseeing your objections. The proposition appeared to him promising, and he immediately found the general title to give to these lectures: *Le feuilleton parlé.* But he added, 'Sarcey is my elder in journalism; he is my colleague in the Salle des Capucines. It will be taken ill if the first advances are not made to him; I will accept only after he has refused.' Thus," added the director, "it is a refusal that I have sought from you. I am delighted with the way things have turned; for Lapommeraye will do this work, which he at heart desires, with much spirit and success, and for you I have another scheme. You give us books."

I started.

"Yes, books. There will certainly appear each week, from September until June, a volume of romance, history, or philosophy, which will be worth talking about to the public. You will take it; you will talk of it in our hall; you will thus institute a sort of course of contemporaneous literature."

He scarcely suspected that, in making this proposition to me, he was flattering my dearest hobby. Every man has had in his lifetime a dream which has never been realized; mine was to have in some paper a weekly *feuilleton,* in which I could do for books what I had done for the theatre in the *Temps.*

When I entered the ranks as theatrical critic, there shone some names which were of the highest order: Jules Janin, Théophile Gautier, Paul de Saint-Victor, and Fiorentino, who was, whatever may have been said, one of the masters of the dramatic *feuilleton*. Others still of less degree were Jules de Prémaray, Paul Foucher, etc. I did not conceive the impertinent idea of ever equalling these illustrious writers; I simply made this reflection, which events have proven just: without doubt some wit and talent are necessary in France to win an audience; nothing told me that I had more than others, and, if I had very little, I could not give myself any more by either toil or artifice. But there are other ways of grappling the crowd and gaining authority over it, which are, it is true, slower, but also surer, and which are suited to me, as they exact only a firm, persevering will, an assiduity that nothing checks, and literary probity that nothing can encroach upon.

"I will go every evening that heaven wills to the theatre; I will never speak of a work until I have seen and re-seen it; I will say of it only what I truly think, and if I think nothing of it I will frankly assert that I think nothing of it.

"That I can do; for the will is all that is necessary. It will take me five years, ten years, fifteen years to persuade the public that I speak only of what

I know, and that I say only what I think. But I shall succeed; for I know beforehand that in this path I shall have no competitor. Wit, with us, runs the streets; there is a little talent everywhere; genius, even, is not absolutely rare. What is really rare is energetic, patient obstinacy in one single idea.

"'Constant dropping weareth away a stone,' says a proverb. I will wear away slowly, week by week, drop by drop, a deeper entrance into the confidence of the public. I will never be afraid of fatiguing or boring them; when I have to give them an account of a miserable, rough sketch I will not treat it lightly, taking on airs of raillery; I will bring to it the same care, the same competence that I bring to more important works. Everything is interesting to him who interests himself in it, and I wish to implant deeply in the brain of the reader this idea, the mother of confidence, that I am interested in what I speak of, and that I only speak of it because it interests me, and that I expect to interest him by speaking the truth, the whole truth, and nothing but the truth."

I gave myself fifteen years in which to conquer the public; I required a little more. But I have reached it in spite of raillery and jesting, for which I cared nothing, of which I was even glad; for every time any one joked me upon my fidelity to representations in the smallest theatres, upon the importance I appeared to attach to the thinnest *vaudeville*, or upon the severity of my judgment, "Good!" I said to myself, "my work is progressing. This excellent brother has gained me three months! What a pity that he is so lacking in both wit and style; his article would be more widely read, and would do me more good." I have not had many such chances. I have been more often than belongs to my share, attacked, cried down, scoffed at. I have been almost always treated thus by the hedge priests of literature. One cannot have everything! One would be too happy, if one had to do only with Zolas, or even with Calibans.

This resolute assiduity and probity would not have carried me far, however, if circumstances had not favored me. In literature, as in everything else, a large part must be left to chance. I have had the good fortune to encounter and fill the post of dramatic critic in two journals, whose success apart from my collaborations has been prodigious. In October, 1859, I went upon the *Opinion nationale*, which Guérout had just founded; three months after, the paper printed thirty thousand copies, and was read by all Paris. Chance might have forced me to remain on it; it dragged along for many years after Guérout's death, without the power to die, forsaken by all, forgotten. Doubtless, I should have continued to write for it as a point of honor, not wishing to leave a paper in its death-struggle. The little reputation that I had been able to gain would have been extinguished in obscurity. No one would have paid any attention to the sound of shots fired in that cellar.

I had the opportunity of quitting the *Opinion nationale* for *Le Temps*. My best friends considered at that time that I made a blunder. For the paper that I abandoned was in full vogue and I was commencing to be personally very well liked there. *Le Temps*, on the contrary, had then only a feeble circulation, and was struggling against money difficulties from which it only freed itself later on. What attracted and determined me was not, as many believed, a question of salary. Guérout had offered to increase mine. It was the grave attraction of that sheet, which the whole University read with devotion. It seemed to me that I should be more at my ease in these very intellectual and serious surroundings, to set forth and develop the theories of dramatic art which commenced to bubble confusedly in my brain. It was a hundred to one that I should lose in hazarding this move. When I think of the agility with which I accomplished this revolution, I am sometimes seized with a little retrospective shiver. I played my whole future upon a single throw of the dice. My instinct served me well. In *Le Temps*, I found the large and severe frame which I needed for the *feuilleton* that I meditated writing, and which finally imposed upon the public; and *Le Temps* has become the journal that you know—a leading journal that is read over all Europe.

Such an opportunity does not come to one twice in a lifetime. I did not have the same fortune with the bibliographic *feuilleton* that I was dreaming of. I resolved to apply the same principles to it. I said to myself: The critics who are charged with presenting literary news in the journals and reviews, are numerous; all are men of wide knowledge, high intellect, and some are superior writers. But they do not generally trouble themselves with rendering the public the service that the public expects of them. They nearly all give themselves up to philosophical considerations, or personal fancy, concerning the works of which they have to give an account; some even content themselves with executing more or less brilliant variations upon a book of which they have read only the title, and perhaps a few pages at random.

The old-time criticism of the eighteenth century and of the Restoration, the criticism which consisted of saying to the reader: Here is what there is in the work; here is what is good in it, and here is what is bad in it; you will do well to buy it, or you can pass it by—that useful and narrow criticism has completely disappeared. It is considered superannuated, and, as we say, *vieux jeu*. Well, I am convinced that a large part of the bourgeois public regret it; that an infinite number of worthy people, half literary, loving to read and having the leisure to do so, would be delighted to have a guide with good sense, with taste, and the honesty in which they could have confidence, whose word they could believe.

That would be, thought I, a *clientèle* to win; and I should reach it by the means that served me for the dramatic *feuilleton*: To read with care the books of which I wished to speak; to analyze them conscientiously, in order to put the things themselves before the eyes of the public, and to conclude by rational criticism which would naturally be worth what he who made it was worth. At first I should have only a small number of attentive readers; I should not be discouraged, for I know that nothing serious or durable can be done without much time and patience. Authority is the confidence of others, and no one wins confidence at a single blow. It is won slowly, by being often right and proving that you are right. Perhaps I should succeed better in this now, having already a strongly established reputation for literary probity elsewhere gained.

You cannot imagine the number of journals and reviews in which I have attempted to found this criticism and give myself this influence. I have had no success; a dozen times I have believed myself near it; a dozen times my jar of milk has been overturned upon my head. I seemed to myself like one of these poor big ants fallen into a bowl full of liquid. It climbs obstinately up the porcelain walls, and each time that it is about to touch the edge, a mischievous child fillips it back into the dish, where it paddles; it is not discouraged, it begins over again with an invincible stubbornness, until finally, capable of no further effort, the body floats inert, its legs stretched out and hanging.

Oh! how sure I was, more than twenty years ago, when Weiss founded his paper, the *Paris*, how sure I was that I was going to win the prize! Concerning literary criticism, I mean concerning the manner of exercising it, Weiss had the same idea as myself. We had more than once chatted about it together. As I was writing in his paper three times a week, he said to me: "As far as you can, take the new books that appear for subjects of *chroniques;* when I definitely organize the *Paris*, I will assign you to a weekly *feuilleton*." Unfortunately for me the *Paris*, one of the most original sheets that ever appeared on the boulevard, had more admirers than subscribers.

Weiss, instead of organizing it, was obliged to liquidate it, and the hope I had caressed flew away again. It was for me a great disappointment, for Weiss would have left me free to say anything I might wish. No one was ever less arbitrary; no one was ever more the friend of truth, or felt a greater horror of advertising, whether gratuitous or bought.

I can give, since the course of the talk has led me toward the subject, a very curious example of it, and one very difficult to believe if one did not know how much imagination Weiss had. One day he took me aside:

"Do you feel the courage," he said to me, "to make a new study which will take you six months of your life, if not more?"

"What is it about?" I asked, a little astonished.

"I should like to have, for the financial portion of the paper, an account of the stock exchange given by a man who will say only what he believes to be the truth, who will not allow himself to be bought by anyone. Will you take six months to study these questions, which ought not to be so difficult to comprehend as they are said to be? then I will give you the financial bulletin? You shall do the stock exchange for the *Paris* as you do the theatre for the *Temps*."

Much as I was accustomed to Weiss's flights of

fancy, I looked him in the eyes to see if he were not making fun of me. No, he was very serious; this eccentric proposition was not a joke. I need not say that I declined the honor that he wished to give me, and I believe that by the next day he no longer thought of his project himself; for he never spoke to me of it again. On the other hand, he returned many times to the idea of a bibliographical *feuilleton*. He was so smitten with it that he took the duty upon himself, and it would have been admirably done if, at that time, he had not been entirely swallowed up by politics, those miserable politics which so grievously spoiled his life.

Thus I have seen crumble in my hands, I know not how many times, this hope of mine; the last experience was the saddest. The *Parti National* had just been founded; at the head of the paper were men quite disposed to accord me whatever might please me. I asked for a literary *feuilleton*, and obtained it. I set myself at work with that imperturbable tenacity which is my ruling characteristic. I had loyally warned the directors: "I shall first be read by only a small number among your subscribers; in three or four years I shall be read by all. In ten years, if God lends me life, I shall bring you readers; I shall have conquered authority."

The *Parti National* was a very well made paper,

At the Salle Des Capucines

wise in tone, and moderate in language, whose circulation increased but slowly; I can say, however, that all the readers of that sheet became my readers and were beginning to believe in me. Presto! the paper changed hands, and the poor ant again fell into the bowl, from which, alas! there is no sign of his ever escaping.

The greater number of papers have, for reasons that I need not comment upon here, suppressed not only the book reviews, but even the articles which, under the name of *Variétés*, were the pride of the ancient press. They will not re-establish them for me; I have bidden a sad adieu to the long hopes and vast thoughts of which the fabulist speaks. I had not yet renounced them when the director of the Salle des Capucines came to propose that I should give, each week, my spoken *feuilleton* upon books, after the fashion of Lapommeraye.

It was not the same thing. Ah, no! it was not the same thing! A paper, however little vogue it has, counts, at the least, fifteen hundred or two thousand readers. Many have thirty or forty thousand; some count up hundreds of thousands. The audience at the Capucines, when the hall is full, is composed of three or four hundred persons, and I suspected that the days on which I spoke of books, especially unknown books, it would be only half filled. I should have at the most a hundred faithful hearers, and that would still be a very pretty number, if I could, at each lecture, gather them about my chair. It seemed pretty certain that, during the first six months, I should not have even that number; I should be forced to form my audience slowly, and week by week. But only young people are in a hurry; at my age, one has time to wait. I have confidence in time. I warned the director, who appeared to me to have strong illusions as to the rapid success of this attempt, that the constitution of an audience was a work of patience, and of long patience. He spoke to me of piquing the curiosity of the crowd by attractive titles; of having the posters flame with the names of scandalous books, those of writers about whose names sounded the trumpet flourishes of notoriety. I would have nothing of all that.

"No," I said to him, "with those methods we shall have half a dozen houses and big receipts; but the attraction of scandal dies out, the trumpets of notoriety do not long turn heads; the stock of idlers will soon run out, and we shall have alienated the serious people who will be annoyed by the noise; if they return to us, it will no longer be with confidence; they will no longer be of the faithful. I am so persuaded of this truth, that I do not wish to be paid, according to the custom of the Boulevard des

At the Salle Des Capucines

Capucines, from the returns. I am **too much afraid** that in some pressing **need** of money—we are all subject to it, **alas!**—I might **yield** to the desire for a full house, and sacrifice a good, honest, and moderate work to a book that was making a noise. I wish to put myself beyond all inclination to commit these injustices. You shall pay me a fixed sum; at least I **shall be sure,** when I **choose a** subject, of not being, **unconsciously, led astray by** considerations of self-interest."

Things were arranged as I wished. It was decided that **I should be** absolutely master of my choice of subjects; **that I** should consult only my personal **preferences, without taking account, except so far as** I wished, of the tastes of the crowd.

My man wanted, at least for the first lectures, to **insert** some flashing advertisements in the papers. I begged him to do nothing of the kind. "**I am** not sure of myself," **I said**; "**it is a** hazardous enterprise. *Periculosæ planum opus alcæ.* I **prefer to** begin modestly without so **much fuss.** It is useless **to** arouse the attention **of the** papers. They will never see in a lecture anything but a pretext for more or less witty chaffing. This chaffing would doubtless bring people to me, but not the kind of people whom I aspire **to** attract, and of whom I wish to take possession. I need believers; my contemporaries would send me only sceptics, and one of the forms of scepticism, in Paris, remember, is to never pay for a seat."

"It shall be as you wish," said my director, laughing. "But with these conditions—it is settled?" He gave me his hand, I gave him mine.

"It is settled," I said.

We had chosen Thursday, because it was one of two days of the week on which the Comédie-Française never gave a first night, nor had an important rehearsal. I commenced, then, with neither drum nor trumpet, almost in secret, before a very restricted audience. I continued for sixteen years, without other interruption than that imposed upon me by the closing of the hall during the three summer months. To-day I am still in the breach, though I have been able, latterly, to arrange these lectures a fortnight apart. I have never had very brilliant successes, nor very bad failures; neither the place, nor the audience, nor the subject invite these extremes; it has been a nearly always equal series of serious lectures, of which some merely give more pleasure than others. I must not fail to tell you some curious particulars, because you may draw from them, not the rules of this difficult business—there are, to tell the truth, no rules for this sort of lectures, any more than there are for the others—but indications and profitable suggestions to those who may wish to engage in them after me.

XIV.

DIFFICULTIES OF THE ENTERPRISE

I found myself at once overtaken by a difficulty that I had, indeed, suspected, but the importance of which I had not calculated.

When one writes a literary criticism upon the book of the day, it is not always sure to be read by the public, but it is perfectly sure to be read by the author. I was going to give each week a spoken *feuilleton* under the title of "bibliography." It was a question whether I should have many hearers; I was certain of one at least, the author himself, who listened, concealed behind one of the pillars of the hall; or in default of the author, someone of his friends sent by him to listen to the lecture and give him an account of it; sometimes even his wife or his daughter.

Oh, woman! I find myself seized, in thinking of her, with retrospective fright. The authors, in truth, I have nearly always found easy enough: they admitted, when we chatted together at the close of the lecture, or they feigned to admit, good ground for some of the criticisms, they laid others to differences as to schools. They discussed doubtful points with me, and without appearing to bear me any grudge, they explained to me with a good grace their intentions, which I had misunderstood. We parted with a handshake.

I do not wish to assert that I have never encountered, among those who have passed under my ferule, any irascible, conceited ones whose ill-humor was afterward exhaled in bitter complaints. Yes, I have more than once had to do with crabbed fellows whose temper I have set going in spite of all my oratorical precautions. But I must say that in general I have had only relations of courtesy, formal or amiable according to their dispositions, with the infinite number of writers whom I have picked to pieces.

I remember that one evening, I had to speak of one of the romances of Jules Claretie, to whom I was bound by a warm and sincere friendship. But there is no friendship that holds. It is a principle of mine, in criticism, that there is a minimum of truth to which the public has a right.

"I mean to come and hear you," Claretie said to me that same morning; "can I do so without annoying you?"

"Oh! you can do it," I answered; "not a word

Difficulties of the Enterprise

shall escape me that would wound a legitimate sensibility."

Evening came, I said what I had to say of the work, and the lecture over, we returned, arm in arm, to our hill, for we lived near one another on the heights of the Clichy quarter.

"It was a strange sensation that I have just experienced," he said to me. "While you were analyzing my book I felt myself in a way flayed and torn to pieces. I felt at certain moments a wild desire to interrupt you, for there are points you know, of course, on which I am not of your opinion, and the necessity that restrained me was horribly painful and grievous. The blood crinkled in my veins and buzzed in my ears. I am, however, very glad to have passed through it. I thank you, but I will not do it again!"

"Bah!" I said to him, laughing; "you will become inured."

There were some, and not among the least, who supported this flaying with still more courage, and more even temper. Thus Richepin, every time he was in Paris, came to the quite large number of lectures that I gave upon his romances and poems. They were not always calculated to satisfy him. He talked about it with me without a shadow of wounded vanity, with freedom and zest, conceding at times that I was right, as though he had to do with someone else's work.

I have, in the same way, had Maupassant speak to me of a study that I had made of him and before him. He was as yet little known at that time, and there was only a little clan of us admirers to believe that he would take one of the first places in contemporary romance. I had chosen, as a pretext to speak of him, a rather thin volume of verse and some of his novels. His baggage at that far away period was not yet considerable.

It chanced that I was not in good trim that day. I wished to read two or three of his poems. I read them ill, and I felt that I was reading them ill. I closed the volume brusquely, very angry with myself; and with that excessive familiarity of language to which I had accustomed my audience.

"I do not know what is the matter with me to-day. I read that like a——

> Et d'une horrible toux les accès violents
> Étouffent l'animal qui s'engraisse de glands." *

And I pronounced the word that Delille formerly dissimulated under this poetic paraphrase.

* "And a horrible coughing-fit chokes the creature that fattens on acorns"—whose name is unspeakable in polite French.

There was, nevertheless, an oh! of surprise and revolt.

"Yes," I insisted, "like a pig. I am false to the poet. It is not, Heaven knows! that his verses are worthy of his prose——"

And I started off. Well, I was not tender to those unfortunate poems, and at the close of the lecture, I saw with some confusion that Maupassant, whom I had not known to be there, was advancing toward me, his hand extended, his face frank. He was much amused both by my mishap and my vexation. And as I was excusing myself, he said:

"But no—no—there was truth, and much truth, I know very well, in all your criticism."

With men, above all with superior ones, all went well. I have never been too much annoyed. But the women, the sisters and friends, were, on the other hand, fiercely uncompromising. I nearly always had them at these lectures. The writers themselves, whether from shame, or indifference, or fear, generally abstained from appearing, or hid themselves in some dark corner, and their presence was revealed neither to me nor to anyone in the audience. Often I only learned of it afterward, through some fortuitous indiscretion. The women hardly ever failed to place themselves in the first row, facing my chair, surrounded sometimes by people of their acquaintance. And they!—they are terrible! No praise, however strong, seems sufficient to them; the least qualification pricks them in the tenderest spot of their hearts, and causes them to cry aloud. You may employ all the forms of expression that the usages of a polite language suggest; they feel under this phraseology the point of criticism, and they resist, and they fume; then they abound in unpleasant recrimination.

How many times have I been pronounced a fool or a brute, by pretty red lips. And what is most irritating is that they are generally unintelligent, but their fervor obscures their judgment, and prevents them from entering into the true sense of the lecturer's words. He sets forth a theory without intending any malice. They see in it a subtle fashion of criticising the work of the man they love, and in the evening, at home, they say to him, "You cannot imagine with what fury he tore you to pieces." They see awry through the glasses of their imagination and their prejudice, and to their eyes all is deformed and grotesque. I cannot, unfortunately, support these reflections with conclusive facts. But how many times it has happened to me, learning in an indirect fashion that some author bore me inexplicable ill-will, to cry to myself in an aside: "What a pity that he was not there himself, in person—that

Difficulties of the Enterprise

he did not hear with his own ears what I said of him; that he should know me only through a translation, and such a translation! The most faithless, possible, made by passionate, nervous, and therefore unreasonable beings."

The disciples were no more agreeable. Every time that I spoke of a writer, an acknowledged master of a school, I was sure to have, outside of my usual audience, a certain number of young people, all fanatics on the subject of the master, whom the liveliest evidence of sincere admiration could not satisfy —they themselves went as far as adoration, as fetichism — who flamed inwardly at the least word of reserve, still more of criticism.

As I am very near-sighted and cannot distinguish faces, I did not see their irritation; but the lecturer is warned by a seventh sense, of the disposition of his audience. An invisible fluid wafts him the sympathy or anger of his listeners. He is bathed in it, so to speak. He feels it through all the pores of his quivering skin. It is a phenomenon which I have never been able to explain, but which occurs too frequently to be doubted. Dramatic artists have experienced it a hundred times. When the curtain rises, even before the hall has manifested its secret inclinations, a puff of warmth or coolness, that rises from the orchestra and strikes them full in the face, warns them of what they have to hope or fear from the audience.

How many times I have set my face against a reserved ill-humor that showed its discontent only by a sullen silence! How many times I have turned it around and around, seeking the place by which I could seize the porcupine, rolled into a ball, to turn aside its prickles and penetrate it. Useless care! trouble lost! Disciples are, for other reasons and in a different way, as intolerant as the women. It is the intolerance of fanaticism.

Thus it was necessary, ceaselessly to adjust one's self to those particular auditors, who came each time to impose themselves upon, or, rather, to annex themselves to, the bulk of my usual bourgeois audience, more animated, more stirring than that, and at times sufficiently numerous and compact to force upon it their preferences or antipathies. It was an egg-dance that I was obliged to execute every Thursday evening. I was not at first very skilful in the exercise; I broke, it is true, only the eggs on which I walked, but I broke all of those. Skill came little by little: I observed myself more carefully, I made for myself a vocabulary of attenuated words, of ingenious equivalents, of suggestive reticences, of sly suspensions, and perfidious turns. Nature had bountifully endowed me with *bonhomie* of manner and

Difficulties of the Enterprise

language. I studied myself to find use for them. I got acceptance for the strongest criticisms with the air of letting them escape innocently, as though I did not myself suspect their keenness; and I accentuated their energy by feigning suddenly to perceive that I had gone too far; I tried then, with simulated awkwardness, to catch them on the wing, and the excuses that I made with an extremely embarrassed air turned themselves into new criticisms. I questioned my audience upon a page that I had just read, telling it with feigned *naïveté* that, as for me, I hardly knew what to think of it; there were things for and against it. I contrived that it should rebel when I stated the reasons for—and then, stopping myself with an astonished air, I said:

"Ah! you think so! I should not have believed it! it is useless in that case to pass to the contrary thesis since that is your own. But I fear you may go too far in that direction."

I had a mass of such little dodges, into the details of which it is useless to enter, because they were entirely personal to me, and other lecturers would have some trouble in making use of them. They succeeded with me, because, so to speak, they fitted into my manner, because there appeared to be no preparation about them; and in truth there was none. Boileau somewhere confesses to us that he does the most malicious things without any malice. I resembled Boileau in that. None of these little scenes were premeditated by me; I should even have been very much embarrassed to tell whether I played them more for myself or more for the audience. When the comedy was actually begun, they flowed so easily, they seemed to me as to others so much the natural expression of my thought. It must be added that I had to do with an audience long trained by myself, that comprehended a hint, and winked intelligently when it beheld one of those developments spring up through which criticism conceals itself under a guise of ingenuous *bonhomie*.

I recall, *à propos* of this, a very witty response once made me by a society lady, with whom I was chatting one evening after the lecture. She, with her husband, had done me the honor, the preceding year, to follow my Thursdays at the Salle des Capucines with considerable assiduity, and I had become acquainted with both of them. The following winter I saw her only at long intervals, and by a fatality that I could not explain, instead of choosing the lectures in which I spoke of fine books that I loved, when I was sometimes very brilliant, enthusiasm being a lively spring of eloquence, she arrived on her husband's arm only on those evenings when the programme contained some work of which she well

Difficulties of the Enterprise

knew, knowing my tastes, I should find it impossible to say anything good.

"Dear me, madame!" I said to her, after one of these lectures, "how sorry I am not to have had you and your husband for auditors last Thursday instead of this. What can you expect one to get out of such a work? I must take it because it has just appeared and nothing else is talked of; but it is against my will. You always come on such evenings. Allow me to regret it."

"But I do it on purpose," she told me; "what need have I to hear you speak of a romance by Zola or Daudet? I have read it myself and I know in advance what you will think of it. But there is nothing so amusing as to see you skirt about a book that displeases you. You have ways of carefully and awkwardly putting your foot in it that are the most enjoyable things in the world. You do not yourself suspect what inflections your voice takes when you read a passage that you consider bad, and which social obligations force you to praise. You have such piteous and forlorn notes in your admiring tone, that when one is used to your lectures it is a joy to foresee them and hear them. When you embark on one of those phrases, full of artful simplicity, which end in either a pin-prick or a stunning blow, a smile plays about the lips of a certain number of the faithful.

And then with you there are unexpected outbreaks; you let yourself go! you have your moments when you are carried away, and then!——"

She spoke the truth. It is vain to keep watch over one's self and hold one's self severely bridled; occasions always present themselves when the depths of nature surge vehemently up and crack all the surface. There is something of Alceste in me, an Alceste eager for brutality, that I have conquered only after infinite trouble, and of which I am not always master. He has done me ill turns in my Monday *feuilletons*; you may believe that I have more than once been his victim in the Thursday lectures.

I recall one day—yes, I must tell you this anecdote, for it is very typical and contains a lesson. All Paris knows M. Vallery-Radot, one of our most brilliant political writers. When M. Vallery-Radot, after his years of study, published his first volume (its title escapes me), I had the good fortune to be one of the first to speak of it, and to present the author to the public. He was grateful to me, and came to thank me. I beheld a charming young man, of very correct bearing, exquisite manners, soft voice, whose conversation abounded in polite phrases, pleasing compliments, but all without a suspicion of coarse flattery—easy and graceful. He pleased me much; I made him very welcome, and urged him to come again. He did not fail to do so. The year after he brought me a new volume in which, telling the story of his student life, he had tried to paint the Latin quarter as he had seen it.

"Very well, I will read it," I said to him, "and rest assured, the article will not be long in appearing."

"This time," he said, "I would ask a little more. I wish that you would take the book for the subject of one of your approaching lectures."

One of my principles was never to pledge myself to give a lecture upon a book without having previously read it. There are, in truth, some books otherwise excellent, from which it would be impossible to make a lecture. A lecture is an hour of speaking, and so many things are said in an hour! The volume chosen must furnish the material, and one or two bits must also be taken from it in which the work is summed up, and which give a just idea of the author's style. I had already been caught two or three times in imprudently pledging my word, and I had had reason to regret it.

In this case, however, I saw no difficulty in promising what was asked of me. Supposing the book were not of the best, the subject itself was interesting. The student of to-day compared with the student of former times! I could always fall back on Castor and Pollux, on Henry Murger and Vallès. And then the young man was so polite, so interesting! He had just married M. Pasteur's daughter, and he had intimated that this would be a way to make myself agreeable to the illustrious *savant*, who was one of the purest lights of our *École normale*.

"Very well, be it as you like," I said to M. Vallery-Radot. "You can count on me. I do not know what I shall say of the book, as I have not yet read it; but the subject of the next lecture must be furnished this very morning; I will put it on the programme."

And he shook my hand.

I commenced to read the book. M. Vallery-Radot had been brought up by the good fathers of the Church, and he had retained a lively and profound gratitude toward them. Heaven forbid that I should blame him! Only, he had in their school contracted habits of reserve and courtesy which may be a supreme distinction in a salon, but which enervate the thought and spoil the style when one carries them into the observation and painting of customs. Doubtless there were in this work curious details concerning the life of the student of this generation, but there was also such an evident determination to find everything good, to distribute eulogies and compliments among the free-thinkers, as well as among the

Catholics, to avoid every dangerous or unpleasant image, every offending word, to roll his words in the honey of amiable phraseology, that I was somewhat irritated. One point especially amazed me: woman was absent from the volume! No women in the Latin quarter! Oh, nonsense! No dancing either! then nothing, indeed nothing!

"Ah!" I said to myself, choking, "the students of to-day are no longer susceptible, then! Is it turnip-juice that runs in their veins? Who has made such young people as that? They are nothing but curled dolls!"

And though boiling with indignation, I still said: "Gently! he is very nice, after all, this Vallery-Radot; there is talent in his book; care should be taken not to wound him who has wounded no one. It will be better to pass very lightly over this criticism, to simply indicate it in a word, and to pause only at the parts where, in recounting what he has seen, he has blocked in the contours with a pencil less vague and soft."

I was thus armed with the best resolutions when I mounted to my chair. I had decided to restrain myself, and I even whispered to myself that it would be quite pleasant to open a box of sugar-plums with this confectioner. I commence, and naturally I begin with this little bit of criticism, reserving all the rest for praise and sweetness. I feel a certain resistance in the audience, and I insist without bitterness or malice; the coolness becomes accentuated. I might have glided quickly over it, and spun along; but suddenly, I know not how, the taste for combativeness which is at the foundation of my character awakes in me; I yield to my temperament, and there I am, like a runaway horse, kicking at random, stamping with transports of anger or outbursts of contemptuous delight: The young people too correct, the phrases too neatly trimmed, the manners too formal, and then, the propriety, the cant! and from time to time, perceiving the devastation that I was sowing broadcast, I stopped—I tried to collect myself; it was only to start off again the more furiously. Nothing remained of the unfortunate book and its poor author.

When it was over and I rose, heated with the galloping charge I had just made, I saw M. Vallery-Radot advancing toward me, a smile upon his lips. He thanked me with the kindliest courtesy for the excellent lesson I had just given him with so much *verve*, and taking me by the hand, he said:

"M. Pasteur has expressed a desire to know you. Will you permit me to present you to him?"

"What!" I cried, astounded. "M. Pasteur was there?"

Difficulties of the Enterprise

"Certainly, and my family, and my friends. I have brought everyone to you."

The roof was tumbling about my head. What folly in me not to have foreseen this audience, or, at least, not to have guessed it from the resistance I felt in the hall. And I had tried to vanquish it, to overcome it by main strength! I could never get over my foolishness. I allowed myself to be led to M. Pasteur, like a condemned man to the guillotine. He welcomed me very graciously; we chatted some moments.

"I assure you," I said to him, when I had recovered my natural manner, "if I had known I had you for an auditor, I should perhaps have said the same things, but I should have said them differently."

He smiled and said, with a shrewd air:

"They would, I think, have gained by being said differently."

M. Vallery-Radot had the good sense to bear me no grudge; our relations remained none the less cordial.

I have not always been so fortunate. I have made some desperate enemies through these scoldings.

I recall the story of a very worthy man, whom I do not wish to name. He belonged to a high government office, and occupied his leisure with making verses which were neither better nor worse than many others. He had published a volume, and was burning to have it talked about. A friend who had just rendered me a great service, and of whom I asked what favor I could do him, begged me to speak of this collection. "All right!" I said. "I am willing; but I will put him with another poet in order to fill up the lecture. They can divide it between them."

"As you like, provided you speak of it."

When the unfortunate man learned that his verses were going to be read and commented upon in public, he could not contain himself with joy.

In his office they rallied him freely upon his hobby, and affected not to believe in his talent.

It was a rehabilitation for him. "The day of glory has arrived!"

He took, unhappy man, a hundred tickets that he paid for out of his own pocket; he distributed them among his comrades and his family.

"You shall see," he said, "you shall see!" And he placed himself in the midst of his battalion. I knew nothing of these details; I was somewhat astonished when I entered the hall to see so many people in it.

Generally, when I spoke of poetry, unless the name of Victor Hugo gleamed upon the posters, I had but a meagre audience; I attributed this increase of curi-

Difficulties of the Enterprise

osity to the other poet, who had made a little name for himself, and I did not further disturb myself about it. I read a number of his verses and read them tolerably well, with strong praise, delaying as long as I could the moment for the arrival of the hero of the occasion, my friend's *protégé*, with whom I had found, as the saying is, nothing to fry.

An "ah!" of relief and curiosity rose from the whole hall. Among the pieces of which the volume was composed, I had chosen one which seemed to me more apt than the others to please my audience, and also easier for me to praise. After some kindly words upon the idealistic tendencies of the book, I undertook the task of reading this morsel. But it is a severe test of a poet to read him aloud. When one reads the verses to himself in the chimney corner, a general harmony that cradles and caresses the imagination, often suffices to charm him. But reading aloud reveals all the weaknesses, it accentuates the error of an inappropriate term; it unfastens the bolt which is left unguarded; if the idea is not strong or just, if the sentiment is not true, the voice of the reader, which brings out in clear relief each member of a phrase, brings out also with cruel clearness the poverty or falsity of the developments. It becomes impossible to mask these failings by a skilful artifice of diction.

In proportion as the reading advanced I felt more keenly the emptiness of the thing; I noticed in front of me, in the bays, a light sound of ironical applause. Ah! irony—there it was! I could not mistake that, the seventh sense, you know; I stopped, and in my good-natured tone, which this time was not assumed, I said:

"Yes, you are right; it is not as good as I thought, but I have noticed others. This is not, perhaps, the best."

I turned some leaves, stopping at one page, from which a mark on the margin signalled me. I ran it over rapidly with my eyes; a silence of expectation weighed upon the hall; I was convinced of the impossibility of reading it aloud with any hope of success.

"Well," I went on, closing the volume, "it appears that it was the best. We will stop with that."

And I rose. Little stifled laughs ran along all the rows of seats. I did not know until later the results of this cruelty. The poor man was horribly vexed by the affront which he had sought, and paid so dear for, for his companions to make fun of. It gave him an illness. They invented a by-word for him in his office; when he spoke of anything, no matter what—a picture that he had seen, a dish that he had tasted—if he praised it,

"Is it really the best?" they asked him.

I was truly sorry when I learned what I had done. It was not absolutely my fault, but there were ways enough of sparing this worthy clerk. This long practice in lecturing has been an excellent school of politeness for me. I gradually laid aside what there was biting and savage in my manner. When I re-read my old *feuilletons*, I am frightened sometimes by the horrible and useless ferocity of language that I encounter at intervals. I say the same things now, but in a gentler fashion, and, as M. Pasteur suggested, they gain by being said differently. It is not that the primitive nature does not reappear from time to time, but those brusque thrusts of a brutal style are more and more rare; and I am convinced that, could I only live two or three centuries, I should become perfection; as our fathers used to say, "a little saint in a niche."

Most lecturers, my comrades, who have to speak in public of the work of a living author, will find themselves exposed to this same inconvenience that I have just experienced with them. I urge them to take the precautions, the need of which I have learned after much groping. I have other advice of a more delicate kind to give them as to the fashion in which they must—I mean by that, in which they would do better, according to my belief, to arrange this kind of lecture and manage the developments.

XV.

ON THE MANNER OF GIVING LECTURES UPON BOOKS

In order to undertake a series of lectures upon new books, and pursue it week after week for years, one needs to be armed in advance with a sufficiently large fund of general ideas ; one must possess a doctrine. When one speaks a single time, by chance, of a work that has just appeared, one can depend upon personal taste to judge it by. It is not the same thing when every week one mounts the platform as upon a judge's seat ; there's no magistrate without a code. The thing needs no demonstration, so I shall not insist upon it.

The first question that presents itself to a lecturer —one much more difficult to solve than the greater part of the public will think it, and one which has long tormented me—is to know where to place the exposition of these general ideas. Is it better to open the conference by treating *ex professo* the part of the doctrine to which you propose to link what you have to say of the book? Or is it preferable to begin with the analysis of the book, and arrive at the general ideas only when you have started them up, so to speak, by beating the bush? Do not think this a question of little importance. I have often told you, in the course of these sketches on the art of lecturing, that there are no good lectures without a good plan; that is to say, a just and luminous arrangement of the parts of which they are composed; and the last thing one finds, or, at least, the last thing I have always found, is the plan. Racine is said to have remarked, "I have finished the plan of my tragedy; the play is done." That is, nothing but the writing remained for him, and the execution of that ought to be very easy to an artist who has sure and easy control of his instrument. When the plan of a lecture is fixed, it is as if the lecture were finished.

It would be most logical, indeed, to commence by setting forth theoretical ideas in virtue of which you should afterward criticise the work. Moreover, you may remark that most of the literary criticisms appearing in reviews are constructed in this way. The author first establishes as strongly as he can the principles of the school in which he belongs; then he shows where the book he is giving account of follows them, and where it departs from them; and he winds up with a conclusive judgment, giving first his major reason, then passing to the minor, and ending with the conclusion which is necessarily deduced from the premises. It is the syllogistic method; it is the rational order *par excellence.*

I have been constrained, after a number of unfortunate experiences, to renounce it, and I advise no one to employ it. It is not, believe me, that I do not consider it the best, but it is too difficult and hazardous in practice.

If you have ever tried, however little, to write or speak, you must have perceived that there is nothing in the world more difficult than to express general ideas. They exact a precision of terms, a justness of description, an authority of style, that one attains only after much work and many efforts; they need, moreover, a particular turn of mind not the most common. The development of a general idea is not improvised; perhaps there are some orators, M. Brunetière, for example, who could indeed state a literary theory without preparing anything but the arrangement of the proofs, speaking fluently on the inspiration of the moment. It would be very dangerous to imitate them.

"Où la mouche a passé, le moucheron demeure."

For my part, I have never been able to manage it. I need (and the greater part of my brother-lecturers are in the same predicament), I need to warm myself up little by little, and it is only at the end of several

Giving Lectures upon Books

minutes that I enter into full possession of my speech. What would happen with this ordering of a lecture commencing with a theoretical exposition? I was obliged to express, precisely when I was not yet going, when the exact and picturesque words would not flow from my lips, ideas which admit of neither vagueness nor inexactness in the language through which they are revealed. Ah! how many times—for I long clung to this arrangement through love of pure logic —how many times I have floundered among the developments in which I had involved myself, without knowing how I should come out! Finally, indeed, I made myself understood, but as I never felt at ease myself, I never caused my audience to feel so.

And between ourselves, my audience—I speak of mine, for there are all kinds, and what I am going to say would doubtless be false of the Sorbonne or l'École Normale—my audience is not so very fond of general ideas and theories. I believe, indeed, that if under the analyses and judgments it had not felt the solid doctrine, it would quickly have tired of statements that consisted only of whipped cream and the whites of eggs beaten into snow. But as to this doctrine, it cared nothing for having it defined *ex cathedrâ;* if I found general ideas difficult to express, it found them difficult to follow. One should always begin by laying a hand upon the audience and attracting it. I started out with imposing upon it the task of reflection, which fatigued it, and prejudiced it against me. I gave myself much trouble, with no other result than boring it and alienating it.

I came then, after long and numerous experiments, to reversing the accepted order of logic, to putting clearly and resolutely the minor before the major of the syllogism, to beginning with the analysis of the book. I adopted an invariable formula:

"Gentlemen, we have to concern ourselves to-day with such and such a work of such and such a gentleman." Then followed some words upon the author and his preceding works, if I knew them, and if I had anything good or useful to say of them. And I entered upon the subject at once with the description of the romance, if it were a romance; with the study of the large divisions of the work, if it were a book of philosophy or history; with naming the most beautiful pieces and their subjects, if it were a collection of poems. Oftenest it was a romance or a work affecting the form of romance, since in our time the romance has encroached upon all classes of work and invaded them.

I recounted the romance, then. Do not imagine that it was an easy operation, demanding no preparation. Some of my confrères, people of infinite learning, of wit and talent, MM. Anatole France and

Jules Lemaître among others, hold this task in criticism to be inferior, and they speak of it only with aristocratic disdain. Certainly it needs not a man of genius to give an account of a play one has seen, or a romance that one has just read. It is none the less a very delicate task, that exacts much taste and extraordinary exactness of language.

It is not a question of describing the romance in minute detail; one might as well read it aloud. One has only an hour, and the book never contains less than three hundred pages; some reach five hundred. One needs must choose, and it is precisely this choice that constitutes the arduous and intricate work of the lecturer.

He cannot do otherwise than indicate the general arrangement of the events which compose the story; but preference must be given to the events that most clearly mark the idea of the work, and to the characters that throw most light on this idea. How shall they be distinguished? It is an instinct to be strengthened by use. When one has this gift—it is a gift—he sees immediately, in listening to a play or reading a romance, the scene or two about which the description will turn, the characters that must be put forward, and those to be pushed into the shade.

There is no rule to prescribe, nor even any advice to be given, for the making of this choice. One of Émile Zola's works, in which thirty characters swarm through a crowd of events, all connected by a single idea, cannot be described in the same way as a romance by Daudet, in which the scenes are more dispersed and the characters more inconsistent; or a romance by Maupassant, or by Feuillet, or by Ferdinand Fabre. In each case you must accommodate yourself to the meaning of the work, to the ideas and tendencies of the author; the finger must be placed just on the point from which the light must spring up and spread over all the rest, and to this point you must cling, bringing everything around it with deliberate purpose, cutting away pitilessly the details that have not to do with it, forcing the others forward.

In the account of a romance, clearness does not result from the care with which one spreads equal light over all parts of the story; that would be a diffuse and fluttering light. The only truth is that which is obtained by showing a great mass of light upon what is, or what one believes to be really characteristic of the work, sacrificing all the rest, which is thrown in the shadow.

A very true eye is needed, and consummate art also, for nothing is more difficult than thus to distribute, in the course of improvisation, events and personages, each one according to the importance given it, and the place assigned to it, and leading all toward the central idea of the narrative. I venture to say, and I do not believe that any of my followers will deny it at the risk of being tasked with vanity, I venture to say, that I have given some lectures of this kind that were, in a way, masterpieces. More than once people, having heard me, have come afterward to chat about my chair, and have said to me:

"I have read the romance with which you have just been entertaining us. I thought I knew it; you have revealed it to me."

One of the compliments which I most enjoyed, was the sally that Michel Lévy levelled point-blank at me after a lecture at which he had been present. He had asked me to speak upon some romance, of which he was the publisher. I had been, it seemed to me, very brilliant that evening.

"Well," I said, finding him at the exit, where he was waiting for me, "are you satisfied?"

"Why, no," he answered, in an ill-natured tone that did not seem to me assumed.

I looked at him, a little mystified:

"And why? What is the matter?" I asked.

"Oh, who do you think would buy the volume after having heard your lecture? They would know it better than if they had read it themselves."

He was sincere in speaking thus. I think, nevertheless, that he was mistaken, for those who were present at the lecture did not fail to speak of it at home to their friends and acquaintances, and aroused a desire to procure the book that they might not otherwise have thought of buying.

I need hardly say that in this kind of lecture, as in all others, I had my good and my bad days. Thus, with Zola, I failed absolutely in talking of "La Terre;" I became entangled with the infinite number of characters, and I lost myself in the detail of the events. The narrative was confused, too prolix at the beginning, forcibly shortened at the end. "L'Argent" was just as difficult to talk about. I only rescued the lecture by extraordinary vivacity. But such are the chances of improvisation.

And the general ideas? and the theories? you will ask me; what did you do with them? Where did you put them, having chased them from their legitimate place. Did you suppress them altogether? Deprive yourself of their support?

Certainly not; but I always managed to put them in some corner of my recital. This recital I turned slyly, without appearing to notice it, in such a way that those of the audience who were at all well-informed (and all of my audience were more or less so) should feel them coming and desire them. Then I no longer needed a serious pause for the purpose of making a long exposition of principles. In a few rapid words I sketched one of the great features of the theory; the audience itself finished the development which I was not obliged to make. I often, even when it was one of the general ideas that constitute the foundation of my teaching, and for that reason are constantly returning—I often, even, suspended a recital or quotation as if I were going to start upon a philosophical dissertation; I indicated it with a gesture or an exclamation, and left it; the audience, having the run of these devices, benevolently conspired with the lecturer and smiled intelligently.

I can, indeed, bear myself witness that during the fifteen years of this course, I have never, after the first attempts, made *ex professo* an exposition of principles nor developed a single theory; and nevertheless, I have slowly impregnated my audience with the ideas which were in some sort the marrow of my criticism.

When I reflect upon it, it seems to me that I have brought to the lecture only those methods, the excellence of which in the *chronique* my experience in journalism has taught me. The *chronique* (at least such as I have always written, and still write) consists in philosophizing upon a fact, small or great, of daily life. I once imagined that it would be necessary, first to set forth the principles in virtue of which I criticised the event, to state them, to prove them, to write a short dissertation which I strove to enliven as best I could. At length I perceived that in the *chronique* it was necessary always to start from the fact and rise to the idea; "to mount," as the philosophers say, "from the particular to the general." Better even, if possible, indicate only by an amusing touch, or enclose in an anecdote, the general idea, which is also the generating idea of the article. There was no reason why the method that was good for the newspaper should not be good for the lecture, which is only a spoken paper. But one does not learn the simplest things all at once, and believe me, nothing is simple in art.

Among those who read this, are doubtless some who are preparing themselves to be lecturers. I imagine that the observations I present will appear sound to them, so sound, perhaps, that certain of them will say, "What a fuss for nothing! We knew all that, there was no need of his taking so much trouble to teach it to us." Well, I will wait until they practise it. They will see if the advice is as easy to follow as it seems.

Another question which disturbed me for a long time in this kind of lecturing, was to know if it were well to make quotations from the work of which one is speaking, or whether it is better to speak one's self all the time.

The solution of this problem, which has its importance, depends upon a mass of considerations that must be taken into account. There are books which do not lend themselves to quotation—those by Émile Zola, for instance. Zola proceeds in masses, the development with him spreads over immense areas, from which it is impossible to detach a passage. It would be wronging him to take a page separately, even though it were admirable, and to read it as a specimen of his style. Zola must be taken as a whole. It is, then, of the whole that you as a lecturer must give the public an idea. Otherwise you betray him. I believe I have never read twenty lines of Zola, unless it were some time when I wanted to put my hearers on their guard against certain crudities of language. It was necessary to read these from the book. But they were exceptional cases.

Maupassant, even though he writes in sturdy, firm, and highly colored language, does not gain by being read in fragments. It never would have occurred to me to read a line from a romance of Claretie's or Hector Malot's, or many others, but there are writers who, to use a word of literary slang, "*font le morceau*," Alphonse Daudet, for instance. Confess that it would be too bad not to arrange a space in the lecture for the reading of a page or two of his; it is clear that one should be chosen that will best characterize the manner of the author, and one should know how to lead up to it.

To lead up to the reading of a fragment that has been selected is an art, and a very complex and difficult art. You must manage to make the public desire it; it is necessary, above all, to soften the transition between the tone in which one speaks and the tone in which one is about to read. If the change is too brusque and too violent, I have remarked that the pleasure of the audience is sensibly diminished. I often used an artifice which nearly always succeeded with me. When I had an important bit to read in a considerable work, I made the lecture converge gently toward that bit, upon which I first improvised in my own fashion, trying to reproduce its movement; then suddenly interrupting myself, I said: "I do not know why I am spoiling an admirable page in this way; listen to the author." And I started off in the same movement, carrying the public with me. You can vary this device in a hundred ways. The essential thing is that you should not arrest the development, which is personal to you, before reading, as a race-horse before a stream that is too wide. You should glide by an almost imperceptible slope from the improvisation to the reading.

There are works, on the contrary, of which you can give the audience a just idea only by the aid of numerous well-chosen readings; thus, a book of maxims and reflections; I have presented many of them to the public—a journal such as that of Goncourt; a correspondence like that of Marie Bashkirtseff, or that of Xavier Doudan. Of those there is nothing to tell; it is necessary to begin with general ideas, by the aid of which you will be able to link together the readings that you will have to give. It is the same with a collection of poems. How do you expect to interest your hearers by praising or criticising for them poems of which they do not know the first word. Here the necessity of reading freely is imposed upon the lecturer. It is for him to choose intelligently, according to the end he wishes to attain; whether he wishes to excite admiration or provoke raillery.

Lecturers who are new to the trade are inclined to think that they will gain success more easily by ridiculing bad verses and jeering at their authors. I can assure them that it is a grave error. The public does not like mockery, and does not long support it.

"Mockery," says La Bruyère, "is often poverty of mind." It does not carry one far. I have always seen my audience smile at a bit of mischief, become amused at a piquant touch; but as soon as raillery becomes prolonged, I have always seen also that it drew away from me, showing uneasiness. It had the air of saying, "If this bit is so detestable, why do you talk to us so long about it? Is it not cruel to insist? Why not pass on to other things?"

The audience (I speak of a lecturer's audience) is pleased, on the contrary, by admiration and gentleness. It likes, when a poem is read to it, to have that poem one with which it can and must be enraptured. There is scarcely a poet of any reputation whose works I have not presented to my audience. I have spoken, I do not know how many times, of Victor Hugo, and even, à propos of new editions, of Lamartine, de Musset, and de Vigny; I have spoken of Auguste Vacquerie, of Catulle Mendès, of Sully-Prudhomme, of Leconte de Lisle, Richepin, Coppée, and twenty others. It is only the poets of the new school that I have not ventured to lecture upon. And do you know why? It is because I hardly ever like them, and do not always understand them. I should be obliged to read them in a way to make their defects felt, and as the criticism would occupy nearly all of a lecture, I should be sure to weary the audience, were it the most intelligent in the world.

If I have any advice to give you, it is, choose for speaking of them in public only the poets with whom you are sympathetic, and choose for reading from their works only the bits that you sincerely admire.

Do not think, however, that it is sufficient for a fragment to be very beautiful to succeed in a lecture. There are masterpieces from which you will draw absolutely nothing. Get it well into your head that a poem, from the moment that you take it from the volume to read it to the public, must have some of the qualities of a drama; it must, as we say, pass over the foot-lights. There are verses that are charming, delicious, exquisite, everything that you choose, but which are made to be read only to two people, or at most to three or four. It is chamber music that must not be transferred to a vast stage. I recall that one day, at the inauguration of a statue of Corneille at Rouen, Sully-Prudhomme wrote with his delicate pen a piece of verse that was a jewel of fine gold artistically wrought. I had read it in the text, and had found that it was really a masterpiece. Mounet-Sully recited it. He sent it forth in a full voice, and with what marvellous art of diction! It left the immense audience that heard it unmoved. It was because the audience was immense, and Sully-Prudhomme is the poet of seclusion.

Victor Hugo, with his flaming and sonorous verse, hits the crowd; Coppée is delicious to read before a small audience like that of the Boulevard des Capucines. Still, with Coppée it is necessary to choose. Not everything will go. Instinct alone will guide you in the choice that you will have to make. Do not allow yourself to be prejudiced by your personal tastes, your individual admirations. Always ask yourself beforehand what the audience will think of the piece that you read. It is not at all through fear of disappointment for your *amour-propre;* it is because if you take from a poet, with the hearty intention of making it admired, a piece of verse demanding mystery and the chimney corner to be understood and enjoyed, you will arrange a failure for him, and betray him. If by chance you are embarked upon a lecture from which you had hoped great success for the author, and you feel that the audience is indifferent, even hostile, do not hesitate to stop short, and, if you are in the humor, take that attitude of your hearers for the text of a lesson, that is always entertaining—I have done it at least ten times—explain to them the reasons for your choice and for their ennui. Take five or six verses—the best ones of the interrupted poem—show that they are charming, and why they are charming; show that they have not charmed the audience, and how it comes that they haven't "passed the foot-lights." Nothing entertains an audience like being blamed in that way, you can turn it like a glove.

I have no advice to give you as to your way of reading the passages that you have chosen. Advice as to that is not of much use. To read is a gift and an art; if you have not received the one from nature, if you have not acquired the other by practice, what do you expect me to say? Better not meddle with it. There are, however, some observations that I have made on this point that will be useful to you, keeping you from dangers over which I have often stumbled.

Consult your voice; I mean by that, pay attention to the quality of your voice. Never, unless from absolute necessity, choose anything to read that does not suit your voice. I possess a very frank, very clear voice, of a slightly sarcastic tone; it is impossible for me to render passages of feeling and tenderness with which a deep, grave voice would do marvels. I know it, and I never venture to read them in public unless circumstances exact it. Then I am always careful to forewarn my audience that I shall give them the meaning, but not the sentiment, of the thing. All the science in the world is helpless against a natural defect, and I defy the most skilful artist to draw from a little fife the moving notes of a violincello.

Never read too long an extract. You, a lecturer, will not gain the same forbearance that is shown the artists, who obtain listeners or feigned listeners even when they recite enormous poems demanding very earnest and sustained attention to be understood. The lecturer's audience is not capable of such attention as that. If, however, you have to read an extract that is rather long and difficult to get at, I will tell you how I go about it. It is another trick peculiar to me, but it seems to me to be within the power of every man who speaks. I saturate myself with the idea or ideas that the poet has expressed (it is nearly always Victor Hugo, many of whose pages, admirable as they are, are nevertheless often abstruse), and without appearing to notice it, I treat them as a subject of a lecture, being careful to insert in my improvisation some of the terms or turns the meaning of which has appeared to me the most difficult to grasp. I thus prepare the task for my hearers. When I open the volume the subject has already become familiar to them, and the principal difficulties of the text are smoothed away. It is a great relief to them, for they no longer have to take the trouble to understand the ideas and connect them.

I then advance slowly, and so soon as I perceive a suspicion of fatigue at the end of a paragraph, I pause under one pretext or another—sometimes to put forth a more or less *prud' hommesque* reflection, sometimes to cry out in admiration over a verse or a word; in reality to give the attention of my audience a rest. It costs me nothing to speak a commonplace: the important thing is to manage an *entr'acte*. I then start off again, and thus arrive, step by step, at the end of the poem. I have, thanks to this skilfully handled artifice, made women listen, from the beginning to the end, to a quantity of philosophical poems which they never could have read at one sitting.

When I have chanced to let myself be carried away by the beauty of a poem, neglecting these precautions, I have left the audience, which could no longer keep up with me, lagging behind. I remember one evening when I had chosen that admirable poem, "Plein Ciel." I was accustomed in this kind of lecture not to mark out for myself the stopping-places. I trusted to my familiarity with the audience. I paused as soon as it showed any fatigue. All went well during the first half of the poem; but once started, I escaped from myself. I paid no further attention to the audience that faced me, and I read solely for my own pleasure, with a very ununusual intensity of emotion and vivacity of manner —better, perhaps, than I have ever in my life read anything else. But alas! the audience deserted me. I ran ahead like a locomotive that spins along without suspecting that the train behind is separated from it and remains in distress upon the road. I only perceived the accident after the lecture was over, in the constrained attitude of my followers, who, seeing me start off so vehemently, had let me go by myself.

Some lecturers, and among others a woman lecturer, Mme. Ernst, have assured me that they had had their audience hanging upon their words while reciting the longest and most abstruse of Victor Hugo's poems. They have had better luck than I, and I don't know how they go at it. You will tell me that doubtless it is because they read much better, with more force and variety. That is possible, though I chance to have heard some of them, and you know I am acquainted with my audience. If I had spoken in such a way it would not have been at the fiftieth, but at the twentieth, verse that they would have parted company with me.

I know only two or three actors in Paris with whom I would not venture to compete in reading aloud. And I have, moreover, the advantage over them of an artifice that I recommend to all my colleagues. Actors, when they recite a poem, remain, and are obliged by circumstances to remain, impersonal. They do their best to render the poet's idea without letting their own emotions be in any way suspected. A lecturer has the right, when he reads a fine passage, to give to his voice the note

Giving Lectures upon Books

of admiration, of enthusiasm, or even of emotion. He has not only to interpret the poem, but, in a way, to herald it. The admiration vibrating in his voice is communicated to the listening public. You know that all sentiment is contagious. All true sentiment, be it understood; for if the audience suspects you of a shadow of pretence, it revolts and treats you as it would a bad actor. You can only save yourself from ridicule by sincerity. But if you act in good faith, with loyalty and skill, you will win effects that will astonish yourself. I have often been able to read the same passage three times over, insisting more each time upon the fine places with a vibration or trembling of the voice, like a man overcome by enthusiasm. Need I add that these effects wear out and fall into discredit by too frequent repetition?

And now, having told you what you must read, and how you must read it, I can only conclude by this last counsel: whenever it is possible, refrain from reading in a lecture. You can keep your audience under better control when you have your eye upon it. The time needed for looking up a paper or opening a book at the right page, the necessity of lowering the head and interrupting the magnetic current established between you and your hearers, the change of tone which is inevitable in passing from improvisation to reading, all contribute to separate you from the people who are in the humor to listen to you. Whenever quotations are not imposed upon you by absolute necessity, speak without paper or book, and in case you have a passage to call attention to, indicate it, even though you murder the text when your memory serves you ill.

The excuse for reading will be still more limited if you speak upon a large stage, or in an immense amphitheatre, before a very numerous audience. It will amount to an interdiction in this case. The more considerable the audience, the greater the necessity of dominating it; and to take a book in your hand is to loosen your hold on the audience.

There, I am at the end of my task. I do not wish, however, to leave the readers who have accompanied me thus far without telling them in what condition the lectures of the Boulevard des Capucines are now, and what has become of lecturing in general in Paris. That will be matter for a short chapter.

XVI.

DECADENCE OF THE LECTURES OF THE BOULEVARD DES CAPUCINES

These Thursday lectures at the Boulevard des Capucines did not escape from the common law which wills that every institution, after a longer or shorter time of prosperity, shall dwindle and enter upon its period of decadence. It had taken me some years to form a quite numerous and very faithful audience. It slowly disintegrated under the influence of causes of which I prefer not to analyze all, because I am writing my own memoirs, and not those of other people.

All that I can and wish to say is that the spirit of the institution, from which my lectures arose, altered little by little, and the directors who succeeded one another at the Capucines, tired of seeing no moneyed success answer to their efforts, abandoned day by day the serious style which did not offer sufficient attractions to the general public, and directed the lecture in new paths. Among those who had, with myself, contributed from the start to impress upon the lectures of the Boulevard des Capucines a character of amiable severity, some grew weary. M. Flammarion no longer spoke, except at rare intervals; Frank Géraldy, who had a marvellous art of explaining in a simple, clear, and animated style the discoveries of contemporary science, retired, occupied with too absorbing functions; Lapommeraye, with whom I had always walked hand in hand, had been appointed professor at the Conservatory, and he seldom appeared in the Boulevard des Capucines.

These were terrible gaps. We now had few save passing lecturers, of whom some, doubtless, were full of learning and talent, but who by a natural self-consideration, having to speak but once or twice, sought rather to win the public by the singularity of the posters or the sensation of the day. They were doubtless right, since, after all, the most important point for a lecturer is not to have to commence before rows of empty chairs. But these were new ways, which frightened away our faithful auditors. In the Boulevard des Capucines, as in a newspaper, as in a theatre, there was a solidarity between us all, and every change that occurred in the customs of the house affected me in the little corner where I moved alone. I no longer felt at home, and my audience itself, stirred by some vague uneasiness, no longer received me with the same sympathy and good-humor.

I had done all that I could to check this little revolution. Every time that I ran across anyone, among my contemporaries of the press, whom I believed capable of leading the literary bourgeoisie toward the Boulevard des Capucines, I begged him to come to its aid. How many entreaties I have made of Jules Lemaître, of Émile Faguet, of Brisson, the acute critic of the *Parti national*, and the manager of the *Annales politiques et littéraires*, and of many others! Unfortunately, lecturing at the Boulevard des Capucines brought but little money and little fame; it was a considerable, even an enormous task, without hope of returns. One could draw from it no other recompense than the honor of having aided in founding a useful institution in France. The prospect was not the most engaging.

I was, in fact, obliged to say to those whom I urged to join me: "You will at first have but a very small number of auditors, you will not receive a cent, and if the papers take any notice of you, it will be only to make fun of you." They all received me with a shrug. Meanwhile, the managers on their side made great efforts in another direction. They invited all the actors who were in the humor to appear upon this new stage; they added the execution of fragments of music to the musical lectures; they brought singers, they organized soirées at which two orators should respond to one another; they invited magnetizers, they were delighted when an adept of the new schools promised them a galloping charge against the old fogies or the old theories.

I do not blame them, Heaven forbid! but you can imagine how out of place I appeared when I arrived, quiet and serious, with my eternal first phrase: "Gentlemen, we are to-day to occupy ourselves with such and such a book." I was the representative of another age, they listened to me as though I came from Pontoise.

I thoroughly understood this situation. I asked the management to no longer count upon me for a weekly lecture. It was arranged that I should put them further apart, that I should not give more than two a month, unless there appeared between the lectures some work that solicited the attention of the public. That was the end of the Thursday lectures as I had conceived them. They formed in my idea an ensemble of teaching, a course of literature for the use of society. I contented myself with being only a virtuoso who came from time to time to execute upon a fashionable theme more or less brilliant variations. I am not altogether that, but if I have kept some little of the old bearing, it is through deference to some half-dozen persons who have obstinately followed me through these evolutions, and who lifted to me a gaze full of reproach if I broke too openly with their ideal of former times.

Last year the manager of the lectures came hastening to me. "I am come," he said, "to propose to you a subject of which the announcement alone will fill the hall. You will see what returns there will be!"

I trembled, for when he put forward a question of returns I was sure that he was going to speak to me of a book of disrepute. I was mistaken in my apprehensions. M. Drumont had just published his second work against the Jews. It was this book that he begged me to have put upon the posters. "As good luck has it," he said, "you have lent a hand to the Jewish cause in the papers. They will all come in the evening."

"If I should accept," I said to him, "there would certainly be in the hall, besides the five hundred Israelites of whom you speak, four or five persons, my followers of old, in whose esteem I should be lowered, and who would perhaps never come to hear me again. They would rightly think that a pamphlet by M. Drumont was not literature. I am not acquainted with them. I only know their faces; they are my conscience."

"But you can say just what you please."

"I understand it thus, indeed, but I have accustomed the public to expect only lessons in literature from me. They will take it very ill if, in order to attract people and gain a little more money, I should throw myself into polemics."

And I refused.

They then left me master of my subjects; but I no longer treat any but those which, while they please me, are of a nature to pique the curiosity of the crowd. So my lectures are more rare, and I continue them only in order not to interrupt the perpetuity of the tradition.

M. Bodinier, at the Théâtre d'Application, has also tried to found an institution of bi-weekly lectures, which are addressed rather to society people, and are given between three and half-past four o'clock, just before the hour for five o'clock tea. The institution is still new, and it is rather difficult to foresee precisely what it will become. Up to the present time it has succeeded. M. Bodinier knew, thanks to the position of general secretary which he long occupied at the Comédie-Française, the greater part of the noblemen and rich men, Tuesday and Thursday subscribers. Many have subscribed to one or two seats for his afternoon lectures, so there are some returns assured in advance, even though the audience be small. He has addressed himself to the most celebrated among us to obtain these lectures, or rather these weekly chats, and I have seen some new names produced. I need not say that I have had my share in this concert.

What induces me to believe that these lectures will deviate from the spirit that animated them in the beginning, is a fact that is small enough in itself, but which in my opinion has important consequences. You doubtless remember with what rapidity the name of Yvette Guilbert emerged from the café-concert, and how the young divette suddenly came into vogue, and a vogue as amazing as it was sudden —such as one sees only in Paris, the land of infatuations.

Mlle. Yvette Guilbert could only be heard at the café-concert, where she sang across the cigar smoke. It was very difficult for good society to venture into such a place. Bodinier had an inspiration. His hall was of the prettiest, his public of the most aristocratic. He engaged the fashionable divette to come and sing her sweetest songs there, and he flanked her with a lecturer charged with explaining her sort of talent, and whose presence prevented, by an air of gentle and learned gravity, whatever effect of scandal this intrusion of pert singing in the Théâtre d'Application might have had. He made a happy hit in his choice of a lecturer. He took Hugues Leroux.

The readers of the *Temps*, of the *Revue Bleue*, and of twenty other papers, were perfectly well acquainted with Hugues Leroux. They were able to appreciate the restless subtleties of his taste, and the fleeting graces of his style. As speaker he is even more winning than as writer. He possesses a voice of penetrating sweetness, which allies itself marvellously with the melancholy of his countenance and the graceful languor of his person. He is, like all nervous people, none the less sturdy and resisting; under the amiability one feels the manhood; there are stores of energy within this frail envelope.

Hugues Leroux acquitted himself with infinite tact and charm in the delicate rôle that he had accepted. He distributed about the fragments Mlle. Yvette Guilbert was to sing, just enough ideas to excite expectation, and these ideas he presented gracefully, without appearing to attach too much importance to them; but also without appearing to hold them too cheap. He kept an exquisite measure between the explanation and the lesson, his sole aim was to please after the divette, and he pleased. Lecturer and singer, the one announcing the other, were a great success, that had to be repeated twice a week to the end of the season.

It is, alas! the most fatal blow ever dealt the lecture. People will no longer come to hear it for itself.

How content do you think the crowd, to whom Rosa-Josepha has been exhibited, would be to see poor Joseph as the only spectacle? Already Bodinier has had imitators. At the Boulevard des Capucines we have seen benevolent lecturers arrange about three or four café-concert songs which were the principal dish, the parsley of their eloquent speech. It is still believed that people who know how to speak are needed for this subaltern duty: it will before long be perceived that the first one who comes along will answer.

He who lives shall see!

I have finished. It only remains for me to make my excuses to the public for having talked so long of myself and of my story. I shall be pardoned, without doubt, if it is observed that in this study I have spoken of myself only to say what I thought of the art of lecturing, and to give the counsels of my long experience to my brother-lecturers.

You can see that I have loved lecturing much, with a love that has not been over-happy. If I turn my head and cast backward a comprehensive glance over these twenty-five or thirty years that I have traversed with you step by step, I see that I have given an enormous amount of work for the slightest possible result; I have tried to found, or rather to acclimate, the lecture in our country, and I affirm that my efforts have been in vain. We have at this moment neither a school of lecturers, nor a public fond of lectures. The lecture has not only cost me time and strength, I have lost a considerable sum in it; for I should have been able to carry into other tasks the prodigious effort of mind, and the incredible number of hours, that I have thrown into that bottomless and echoless pit. Ah! well, I regret neither my time nor my trouble, nor my money. And do you know why? Because I have felt in lecturing a kind of pleasure the equivalent of which I have found only in play—the pleasure of struggling against chance, the terrible and charming sensation of casting the die.

At the end of some years in my calling I could scarcely feel any emotion in writing, I was so perfectly sure that amid the thousands of articles which flowed in a torrent from my pen, there would not be a single one absolutely bad, because I knew my trade to the foundation; that some would be excellent, others good or mediocre, according to chance; but the public would not notice, reading on the fly and judging a man by the ensemble of his productions.

While as to the lecture! I could never be certain in advance that I should not break my neck, and that was delicious. However much assurance the habit of speaking may give a lecturer, he never knows how things will turn for him, and his heart leaps in his breast like that of a player who has put his last five louis on the red. He hopes and he fears! Do you know any greater happiness for a man?

The lecture has given that to me. Had it not rendered me this service, I should still be grateful to it. I am of those who believe that no effort is lost, no labor fruitless. I cannot for the moment see the fruit that I and my fellow-lecturers have gathered during these long and laborious campaigns. But who knows? Possibly the seeds that we have sown will spring up some fine morning. Possibly it may some day produce a more skilful or a happier orator, who, taking up our task, will climb the mast upon which we have slipped, but for whom we have made the ascent easier, and who will bring down the cup. And as for me, my recompense is that the lecturer of the future will hardly be able to do other than open this little volume, were it only for the sake of its information, and that he will say, after having run it through: "He was a good fellow and a hard worker; he knew what he was talking about, and he was not so altogether stupid as the *beaux esprits* of his time would like to make out."

I ask no other funeral oration. You see I am not ambitious.

NOTES

P. 4. ÉMILE DESCHANEL, born at Paris, 1819. Professor in the École normale and dismissed for anti-Catholic criticism in 1851, he entered journalism as a liberal, was imprisoned and banished after the Coup d'État, and took up the work of lecturer in Belgium. Readmitted to France in 1859, he joined the staff of *Les Débats*. He is the author of numerous anthologies, accompanied by piquant personal comments: "Les Courtisanes grecques," "Le Mal qu'on a dit des Femmes," etc. He was elected to the Chamber in 1876 as a Republican, and in 1881 was elected a life-Senator. He has published since a number of critical works, including a life of Benjamin Franklin.

P. 5. JEAN-BAPTISTE ALFRED ASSOLANT, born at Aubusson, 1829. After a brilliant career as professor, he resigned after 1851, and made a long journey in the United States, the fruit of which was found in numerous sketches, half-philosophic and half-humorous. He has since been an active journalist in politics, literature, and the drama, but, though essaying three times, has never reached the Assembly.

P. 8. GASTON SOUILLARD DE SAINT-VALRY, born in Eure-et-Loir, 1828, died in 1881. Known chiefly as the literary critic of the *Patrie*.

P. 12. FÉLIX HÉMENT, born in Avignon, 1827, noted for his zeal in the promotion of popular instruction in science, through teaching, lecturing, and books, of which latter one, "Simples Discours sur la Terre et sur l'Homme," was crowned by the Academy in 1875.

P. 17. PIERRE-HENRI-VICTOR BERDALE DE LAPOMMERAYE, born at Rouen, 1839, critic and lecturer. In 1881 was given charge of the course of dramatic history and literature at the Conservatory.

P. 18. CHARLES-AUGUSTIN SAINTE-BEUVE, born at Boulogne-sur-Mer, December 23, 1804, died at Paris, October 13, 1869. Originally one of the romanticist poets, in 1837 he devoted himself to a history of Port-Royal, which occupied nearly twenty years of his life. He was appointed librarian of the Mazarin Library in 1840, Professor of Latin poetry of the College of France in 1862, and Senator in 1865. From 1850, he published a series of weekly articles of criticism and biography in the *Constitutionnel*, the *Moniteur*, and the *Temps*, by which he is most widely known.

P. 32. Father HYACINTHE or CHARLES LOYSON, born at Orléans, March 10, 1829. Formerly a Catholic priest and noted preacher, who left the Roman Church, married, became first an advocate of the Old Catholic, then of the Gallican Catholic Church, and finally connected himself indirectly with the Church of Scotland. His latest work in public was in support of General Boulanger.

P. 33. HIPPOLYTE-ADOLPHE TAINE, born in the Ardennes, April 21, 1828. Philosopher and critic and historian, his chief works are the "Histoire de la Littérature anglaise," various books on art, and the "Origines de la France contemporaine." For some time his liberal doctrines in philosophy kept him from the Academy, but he was elected in 1878. In philosophy he is an evolutionist of the school of Spencer. In politics he is conservative, and held positions under the Empire in St. Cyr and the Beaux-Arts, the latter of which he still retains.

P. 33. JEAN-JACQUES WEISS, born at Bayonne in 1827. Teacher and journalist, he was connected with the *Débats*, wrote for the *Revue des Deux Mondes*, and established the *Journal de Paris* in 1867. He entered the public service under Ollivier, and after the fall of the Empire was councillor of state under the Republic. He became, later, editor in chief of the *Gaulois*. He was a warm friend of Gambetta, and was in the Foreign Office under his ministry. He afterwards undertook the dramatic criticism for the *Débats*.

P. 44. JULES SIMON, born at Lorient (Morbihan), 1814, entered the Department of Education as professor of history and philosophy. He was a Republican deputy in 1848, and councillor of state in 1849. After the Coup d'État he retired to Belgium, but returned to France and was elected to the Assembly in 1863, and voted against the declaration of war in 1870. He became Minister of Public Instruction, Worship, and Fine Arts in 1870, as a member of the Government of National Defence. In 1876 he became Prime Minister under MacMahon, and resigned on the famous May 16, 1877. He was a devoted friend of Thiers, and pronounced the funeral oration at his grave. Apart from politics his work has been chiefly in the department of instruction. He is the author of many works on philosophy and history, and the editor of others.

P. 82. MAÎTRE PETIT-JEAN was a famous doctor of theology of the early part of the fifteenth century, and author of the plea that it "is permissible and even praiseworthy for anyone to kill a tyrant"—an apology for the murder of the Duke of Orleans by the Duke of Burgundy, in whose pay the doctor was.

P. 84. THÉODORE FAULLAIN DE BANVILLE, born at Moulins, 1823, poet and dramatist and dramatic critic from 1869 of the *National*.

P. 84. FRANCIS-ÉDOUARD-JOACHIM COPPÉE, born in 1842, poet and dramatist, author of "Le Reliquaire," "Intimités," "La Grève des Forgerons," "Le Passant." Since 1878 he has had charge of the Archives of the Comédie-Française.

20

P. 101. JEANNE SAMARY, born at Paris, 1859. She made her first appearance at the Théâtre-Français August 24, 1875, where she took the soubrette parts. Among her favorite rôles were *Toinon* in "L'Étincelle," and *Suzanne de Villiers* in "Le Monde où l'on s'ennuie," though she attained great distinction in the classic repertory. In 1880 she married a banker, M. Legarde. She died a few years ago in the fulness of her powers and fame.

P. 101. HENRI DUPONT-VERNON, actor, born at Pulseaux (Loiret), 1844. He entered the Français in 1873, and gained fame as *Laffemas*, in "Marion Delorme," and in classic rôles. In 1888 he was made professor of declamation in the Conservatory.

P. 102. BENOÎT-CONSTANT COQUELIN, actor, born at Boulogne, 1841. He entered the Théâtre-Français in 1860, and became sociétaire in 1864. His greatest success has been in the classic repertory, but his range in modern comedy is very wide.

P. 103. SARAH BERNHARDT, whose baptismal name is Rosine Bernard, was born at Paris, October 22, 1844, and was the daughter of a Holland Jewess. She appeared at the Théâtre-Français in 1862, but had little success. Afterward, at the Odéon, she played *Zanetto* in "Le Passant" of Coppée, and the *Queen* in "Ruy Blas," and was admitted to the Français, where she had a very brilliant career, leaving the company some fifteen years ago for a still more brilliant one in all quarters of the globe. She studied sculpture and painting, and has exhibited works in both arts.

P. 106. ERNEST-WILFRIED LEGOUVÉ, born at Paris, 1807, novelist, dramatic author, notably in collaboration with Scribe, and writer of essays and manuals on elocution.

P. 127. EDMOND-FRANÇOIS-VALENTIN ABOUT, journalist and writer, born at Dieuze (Meurthe), February 14, 1828. In 1851 he was appointed professor in the School of Athens. His first work (1855) was "La Grèce contemporaine," which had a great sale. During the next three years he published "Tolla," a novel largely autobiographic, "Mariages de Paris," "Le Roi des Montagnes," "Trente et Quarante," and many others. He entered the field of politics with his pamphlet on "La Question romaine." During the decade preceding the Franco-German war, he published numerous novels and pamphlets, was one of the editors of *Le Constitutionnel*, *L'Opinion nationale*, *Le Gaulois*, and *Le Soir*. The most famous of his novels was "L'Homme à l'Oreille cassée," a stinging satire on the pseudo-bonapartisme of the Second Empire. After the war, with M. Sarcey, he founded the *XIXme Siècle*.

P. 212. HENRI MEILHAC, dramatic author, born in Paris in 1832. He has been one of the most prolific and successful of writers, both of plays and librettos. His best-known works were in collaboration with M. Ludovic Halévy (music by Offenbach), "La Belle Hélène," "Barbe-Bleue," "La Grande-Duchesse de Gérolstein," "La Périchole," and the well-known comedy, also with Halévy, "Frou-Frou."

P. 236. CALIBAN, pseudonym of Auguste-Émile Bergerat, journalist, novelist, dramatic writer, born at Paris in April, 1845. He is a son-in-law and biographer of Théophile Gautier.

www.ingramcontent.com/pod-product-compliance
Lightning Source LLC
Chambersburg PA
CBHW030748230426
43667CB00007B/888